TAROT
IN OTHER WORDS

TAROT
IN OTHER WORDS

*An Essential Anthology by
Leading Queer Tarot Writers*

EDITED BY

Cassandra Snow

WEISER
BOOKS

This edition first published in 2025 by Weiser Books, an imprint of
Red Wheel/Weiser, LLC
With offices at:
65 Parker Street, Suite 7
Newburyport, MA 01950
www.redwheelweiser.com

Copyright © 2025 by Cassandra Snow

All rights reserved. No part of this publication may be reproduced or transmitted in any form or by any means, electronic or mechanical, including photocopying, recording, or by any information storage and retrieval system, nor used in any manner for purposes of training artificial intelligence (AI) technologies to generate text or imagery, including technologies that are capable of generating works in the same style or genre, without permission in writing from Red Wheel/Weiser, LLC. Reviewers may quote brief passages.

ISBN: 978-1-57863-844-4

Library of Congress Cataloging-in-Publication Data

Names: Snow, Cassandra, 1985- editor.
Title: Tarot in other words : an essential anthology by leading queer tarot writers / edited by Cassandra Snow.
Description: Newburyport, MA : Weiser Books, 2025. | Summary: "This book is an essential collection of writing by leading queer tarot writers and community leaders about their tarot practice and its relevance to LGBTQI2SPA+ [or QUILTBAG], QTPOC issues, and beyond. It offers alternative approaches to reading the tarot for those looking to gain new and deeper insight--especially for marginalized folk who don't see themselves reflected in traditional presentations of the tarot"-- Provided by publisher.
Identifiers: LCCN 2024053891 | ISBN 9781578638444 (trade paperback) | ISBN 9781633413429 (ebook)
Subjects: LCSH: Tarot. | Homosexuality--Miscellanea. | Sexual minorities--Miscellanea.
Classification: LCC BF1879.T2 T356 2025 | DDC 133.3/2424--dc23/eng/20250111
LC record available at https://lccn.loc.gov/2024053891

Cover and interior by Brittany Craig
Cover image © iStock
Typeset in Minion Pro

Printed in the United States of America
IBI
10 9 8 7 6 5 4 3 2 1

*This one is dedicated to all the queers
who blazed their own path
and made us all better for it.*

CONTENTS

Introduction **ix**

PART I
Finding Ourselves in the Tarot

Introduction **3**

The Grieving Fool
by Asali Earthwork **7**

Queerness Has No Timeline: Exploring a Slower Journey with the Magician, the Four of Wands, and the Seven of Pentacles
by Rebecca Scolnick **25**

The High Priestess as Black Femme Memory
by Junauda Petrus **41**

The Empress
by Maria the Arcane **55**

A Life Well Built: Exploring Queer Adulthood with the Minor Arcana
by Cassandra Snow **75**

Queering the Lichens, Queering the Cups
by Maria Minnis **85**

PART II
Finding the Tarot in Ourselves

Introduction **93**

Queering the Questions Themselves
by Cassandra Snow **95**

Queering Tarot's Numbers: Affectionate Alternate Title - "Gay Math: I Know, but Listen"
by Meg Jones Wall **103**

A Secret Third Thing: Court Cards as Queer Elements
by Charlie Claire Burgess **121**

Trick Mirror Tarot: Seventy-Eight Multifaceted Self-Reflections
by Siri Vincent Plouff **139**

A Treatise on Queering Symbols
by Taylor Ursula **155**

And With That . . . **173**

Appendix: Essayist Bios **175**

Cassandra's Acknowledgements **179**

Introduction

My first book, *Queering the Tarot*, began as an article series running on a couple of different blogs. This was way back in the early 2010s. At that time, there was very little explicitly written for queer tarot lovers (or would-be tarot lovers) that addressed the ways our work with the cards deviates from what tarot books typically cover. There was even less that inspired us to use the cards for *all* of our queer desires. Where were the tarot books for those of us who looked at the Devil or the Eight of Swords and saw a saucy and satisfying Saturday night? Or who looked at the World and thought of the ways we wanted to make our world better? These were the stories tarot whispered to me during sleepless nights under the stars. These were the stories I hungered to read when I read about the cards.

It is, after all, through tarot that I came into my own full spectrum of desires. Way back in 2003, I began my tarot journey in, quite literally, a musty dorm room basement. Tarot was very much a midnight exploration with outsider culture friends from our Baptist college's otherwise crushingly conservative campus. The same friends who slipped me DVDs of *Boys Don't Cry* and *The Rocky Horror Picture Show* were the very beloveds who introduced baby queer me to indie twee and alternative music. This chosen family who took me to all the cool hipster spots in the next city over—these were the friends who first shoved a deck of seventy-eight cards labeled simply "tarot" into my hands after a few too many wine coolers (which we were definitely not supposed to have on said campus) one fateful October night in 2003.

I was learning tarot through this lens of discovery, experimentation, and coming alive the way we do in our very late teens and early twenties. Seeing the world through this lens was not only a vital part of normal developmental growth for me but was *necessary* for queer people of my generation to do, especially if we were raised in less-than-perfectly accepting circumstances. The tarot held my hands through absolutely everything I went through as a college student, including coming out of the closet and beginning life all over again. The tarot still holds my hand to this day, whether I am discovering new facets of and words for my sexuality and gender or figuring out how to contribute to movements while physically disabled. The tarot taught me how to truly connect to spirit, to self, and to others, and it is from there that my queerness unfurled and colored everything else for me. It still does this for me, and I have been so blessed to spend the last couple of decades helping other people find the same love and support I found in the cards.

When I started reading tarot, it felt like a secret. It was a mystical thing with a mysterious pull, and it was my job to uncover that arcane language somehow. Viewing this through a queer lens while you are in the closet feels very different than how you view it from the outside of the closet. Spiritually speaking, a secret or a mystery means something you must live to understand. You can't learn about it intellectually or secondhand. You certainly can't process it emotionally or intuitively unless you have been through it. The witchcraft community speaks of mysteries of various genders, but what of queer mysteries? What are the keys to finding a secure place to fully embrace your myriad desires—many personal, many political, many social? What exactly is the lock we're trying to unlock with those keys, and why? These are the questions that mattered to me at eighteen, and they are the questions that matter to me twenty years later. Still, I do not see queerness written about with the frequency or acceptance that other mysterious points of view are in occultist publishing.

By the very nature of sacred mystery, I can't answer any of those questions for you either, but that's also not the point. What I can do is offer you the knowledge and tools I've accumulated in my thirty-eight years of being alive and urge you to find your own way with them. That was always the purpose of *Queering the Tarot*, but when I started thinking of my next moves after *Lessons from the Empress* was published, I knew it wasn't my knowledge and tools alone that would be most useful. I started dreaming of an essay anthology with a bunch of other tarot queers with Things to Say, and the idea for this book grew from there.

When I penned *Queering the Tarot*, there was very little like it out there. Now, tarot is no longer a late—night outsider—culture experiment, and the supposed "niche" of queer tarot readers, thinkers, and writers has exploded in the most delicious way possible. Many of the essayists contributing to this anthology are part of that delicious explosion. Decks by Charlie Claire Burgess and Taylor Ursula have undoubtedly changed the field. Books like Meg Jones Wall's *Finding the Fool* and Maria Minnis's *Tarot for the Hard Work* have forever changed how we look at and think about tarot cards. Even the way we use blogging and social media to build a community of queer cartomancers is changed and shaped forever by things like Asali Earthwork's ongoing Tarot of the QTPOC (queer, trans, and people of color) project.

It is overdue for a book like this to hit the shelves IMQO (in my queer opinion). The ten of us contributing to *Tarot in Other Words* and countless other brilliant people have been in conversation for years about these topics. Now we are delighted to bring these (hopefully) thought-provoking, eye-opening, and queer conversations directly to your bookshelf. I hope you take this collection and read with an open and titillated mind. I hope you use the information, theory, stories, and ideas presented not only to amplify your own tarot knowledge base but to enable yourself to dream it into something bigger, queerer, and more outlandish than you currently think reading tarot ever could be. I hope this book serves as reference, of course. More importantly, though, I hope this book serves as a jumping off point for your own personalized, creative, and deeply thought-out tarot practice.

A Note on Reading Tarot If You're Pretty New to It

Learning any new skill can be overwhelming. Learning a new skill with centuries of history, discourse, and inner-community arguments, especially so. There is a lot of mystique around how to read tarot, and a lot of ideas and interpretations out there. Some of this is fun and interesting. It will become less confusing the longer you stick with learning. For deeper and more personalized readings, you just need to find your "in," which hopefully this book will provide for you.

Please know before we go any further that there are no right or wrong ways to read tarot. What makes for a good tarot reader is someone who is willing to learn, and slowly—and someone who is willing to trust their own intuition and creativity. What you need to develop a tarot understanding is just four things: study, practice, play, and a willingness to engage all three of these aspects.

However, if we are to develop queer understandings of tarot cards, we need to start not with the cards but with naming how *we* define queerness and how it shapes our worldview. Your answer to those giant questions is probably a little (or a lot) different than mine. Hell, my own definitions have changed many times throughout the years. Nonetheless, how you see yourself is also a part of how you view the world around you. This will obviously affect how you read tarot, just as it affects how you take in movies, conversations, or even a landscape in the distance. Knowing your point of view from a place of trusting in your self-knowledge makes your intuitive voice more clear. It also makes you more confident in espousing the things your intuition tells or shows you.

The next question I'd ask you before you start your tarot journey is this: What purpose do you see tarot having in your life? What "is" tarot to you, and why are you choosing this tool to learn? These answers also may shift and change the more you work with the cards, but knowing why you are approaching the cards in the first place will certainly color how you build a relationship with them.

From there you can approach the cards however you like. There are countless techniques to play with. To get you started though, here's an extremely abbreviated process of how I read tarot, whether for myself or someone else.

- ❖ I first like to sit with the tarot card(s) I pull for a few moments before forming concrete ideas about what they are trying to say to me. In these moments, I survey the images and take in what I see in them. I connect the dots between the symbols or images, and naturally begin to get an idea of what this reading might be saying.

- ❖ Once I have some loose ideas, I fold in what I intellectually and spiritually know about what each card can and often does represent. I try to synthesize that with my creative and intuitive ideas from the first bullet point, and usually am able to. Where some people stumble with tarot is that often we are asked to consider multiple truths, multiple options, multiple ideas. It is okay if there are contrasting messages on the table, so long as you're noticing those contrasts.

- ❖ If there are multiple cards on the table, I look at how they weave together or contrast each other to see what that adds to the reading's message.

- ❖ I might also double-check resources if I'm not clear on what the tarot is telling me yet. I might jot down a few words to see if writing them out helps me link them together in some way. I might even try doodling, just to get my brain to open a little.
- ❖ Finally, I scan for prominent symbols or movement in the cards that I may have missed or overlooked and fold those ideas into the other ones that are forming.

Once I follow these steps (though not always in this order), cohesive messages begin forming. These cohesive messages are the meat of your reading!

As I said, there are many, many tarot techniques. This one is very basic and leaves a lot of room for you to add your own distinct flavor as you go. This process can be looked at as a skeleton guide to reading tarot that will help you as you learn and process other ways to read, including the very ones in this book. Try not to get hung up on "right" meanings while you're getting your feet wet, but don't be afraid to use and study your sources as often as you can. Your inner voice should be the strongest one in a reading, but if you want some roots in your practice, it is okay if that's not the only voice informing it. In any case, start small. Ask simple questions. Look for simple answers. Note the colors, symbols, and movement of your cards. Think about what you know them to mean either collectively or personally. This is a great way to get started and begin reading cards accurately before you have any real idea what you're doing.

That being said, critical thinking *is* a really important piece of reading tarot that gets overlooked all too often. It's not enough to know that a lot of red in a card means passion is at play, for example. You won't get a reading out of just that very basic correspondence. What you can do is use that as a jumping-off point for deeper inquiry. Ask yourself questions to arrive at a clearer point. That might mean questions like

"If I asked about a specific situation, and got all this red, where are my passions leading me re: this situation?"

As you work with the cards and begin picking up all kinds of symbolic languages, you should still check in with yourself along the way. In our example, you might later ask, "Is it true to my experience that red means passion? If so, what are examples of that? How has red shown up in my life or not, and what might *that* mean for this reading?" Trust your first instinct—but don't let the entire reading boil down to it. First thoughts are important *to get you heading down the right trail.* The reading is in what said trail leads to or shows you on your route.

As we can see, reading tarot well takes a combination of practice and skill. It takes trusting yourself and investing time and energy into the greater tarot community. It takes thinking and imagination and intuition. We are all absolutely capable of getting there. Give yourself grace, and don't be afraid to mess up. Don't be afraid to play or experiment. *Do* be afraid to set card "definitions" in stone. Leave room to grow. You and the way you'll interpret tarot cards deserve the safer space to evolve. Safer space and room to experiment or feel things out is a lot of what tarot wants to provide for you—so let it.

Why Essays on Queer Tarot Topics?

Speaking directly to (but never for) my fellow queers is always one of my primary interests whether I am making theatre, slinging cards, or writing books. I think embracing queerness can teach us so much about not even just gender and sexuality, but how and why we should liberate ourselves in the first place. I think queerness teaches all of us that who we are is right, beautiful, and sacred. I think that queerness teaches us that what society deems "best" or standard is not the right fit for, really, a lot of people. It teaches us to honor differences in others and understand that what is good for me may not be good for others. I think that the queers I know are, for the most part, the coolest and smartest people I have ever met in my life. So a lot of why this book came about is simply because I wanted it too, for all of those reasons and so many more.

Even so, queerness and tarot do have historical social roots in each other. While common tarot history and myth tell us that tarot officially began in the 1400s primarily for groups of nobles, and while that is true in many ways, there is so much more history for tarot writing to explore. This isn't a history book, but I do want to bring some lesser discussed history and trivia to the table that ties queerness and tarot.

One of the biggest reasons I think of tarot and queerness together is this: For a lot of cultures, such as the Romani and other oppressed groups forced into nomadic lifestyles, fortune-telling using cards and other tools was and is to this day survival work. The same reason we see so many queer or disabled people and BIPOC take up tarot in the United States is the same. We take it up for survival, and to feel as free as we can while we earn money to survive. Of course, not every oppressed person who reads tarot does it for other people. If they do, they may not read for money. Still we are drawn to tarot like it feeds us. In my own life, tarot reading was the career I launched when it became increasingly clear that I was too disabled for a full-time day job. It is literally the work that has kept food on the table. Because of my disability, I didn't just need money though. I needed flexibility. I needed community. I needed to do something that would keep me from becoming a full-time hermit and allow me joy and pleasure along the way.

Survival is so frequently about material goods, but it isn't *just* about material goods. As humans, we need everything else I've brought up too: community, spiritual feeding, creative outlet. Tarot feeds us in these ways and so many more. Tarot feeds our spirit. It nurtures and protects our hearts. It quenches existential thirst when we want to know what it's all for. It makes space. It allows us to breathe. On a practical note, it is an endlessly giving gift for those of us who like having things to think about, mull over, or philosophize about. In other words, it feeds our intellect.

As we move through tarot's history, we see more blatant threads tying queerness and tarot together. While we cannot for sure confirm that Pamela Colman Smith was queer, the rumors are rampant enough to believe them, and she did have a woman who was her "companion and roommate" for most of her life. If you're not sure who Smith is, buckle up to learn more about this early female occultist who illustrated the juggernaut of tarot decks: the *Rider-Waite-Smith* deck. This deck was created by A. E. Waite as an expression of Golden Dawn belief at the turn of the 20th century. It is also the deck most often written about, re-created, and used today. This means the deck most often used for adaptation and learning was illustrated by a queer woman.

Coming closer to present day, Rachel Pollack, the absolute badass of a woman who penned *78 Degrees of Wisdom* (arguably the most influential tarot book in existence) along with many other tarot works that serve as a bedrock of our field, was a trans lesbian doing radical work to legitimize tarot as early as 1980. While her work was limited by the constraints of publishing and society at the time (*78 Degrees* was first published in 1980), her life probably looked very similar to a lot of the queers you know now. That voice and experience do come through in her work, and her work is so influential that, of course, it shows up everywhere now!

Tarot's current renaissance owes a lot of its success to modern-day queers too. Books penned by Michelle Tea, famed queer memoir and novel writer, top the tarot book sales lists alongside Pollack and books about Smith's original work. As tarot was becoming more common, Little Red Tarot, a queer-run and mostly queerly authored community website, was a beloved resource until it voluntarily archived. Queer tarot decks like Cristy C. Road's *Next World Tarot* and Cedar McCloud's

Numinous Tarot are bestsellers. (As is the *Fifth Spirit Tarot* by this collection's own Charlie Claire Burgess.)

These are just a few (admittedly huge) examples of why tarot can be considered inherently queer, but we as queers have always been everywhere. We have existed in every community, in every spirituality, in every niche literary market since the dawn of time. That certainly includes the tarot, and it is high time we talk about that.

The best way to honor queer history is to keep pushing for queer liberation. It is our duty to these queer and trans ancestors (trancestors, if you will) to take our fields and make them queerer. This isn't exclusively true to tarot, but it's true to it nonetheless. Queer ancestors have fought to be seen, heard, safe, and respected since the dawn of colonialism, if not before. We owe it to them to keep going when we are able to do so. Tarot is one of many places where some of us are blessed, lucky, and privileged enough to do just that. Every time we create a queer tarot deck, write about queerness in tarot, or use tarot to help LGBTQ+ people feel at home in their own bodies, we are honoring Smith, Pollack, and all the others who came before us.

On a personal note, to me tarot is inextricably linked to finding, using, and maintaining our voice. Whether you are queer, BIPOC, disabled, or different than your peers in any way that has made you an outsider, you deserve to be able to relate to the tools that give us our voices back. I write and create for people who want to make the world better. I also write and create for people who simply want to figure out who they are and what to do about it. It's worth noting that that is still a form of resistance and of rebellion in a society that wants identical workers to simply clock in, clock out, and then go buy things. You are so often doing your part by just being who you are, even if you can't be out for safety reasons, even if you can't do anything other than simply be. Your queerness is still sacred, and you still deserve the space tarot can carve out for it.

So . . . Who Gets to Call Themselves Queer?

There are few topics in community discourse that I truly care less about than this one, I'll be honest. Queer people are being attacked legislatively, physically, and certainly emotionally and psychically every day. While we are being tormented for our differences in gender and sexuality, you probably know if you are straight or not. You probably know if you are cisgender or not. If you don't know, you are probably questioning, a thing that, frankly, most cisgender and straight people do not spend a lot of time doing. This is the only definition I hold: Queerness is for anyone who is not straight and/or not cisgender. Period. If you fall anywhere under the LGBTQI2SPA+ or QUILTBAG (queer and questioning, undecided, intersex, lesbian, transgender or transsexual, bisexual, allied or asexual, gay or genderqueer) umbrella, you are queer enough.

In my ideal world, queerness is for those who fight for it, that is, those who fight for our dignities, safety, and rights. This means those who resist being anything other than what they are at every turn. It's for those who make safe space for others to explore their own queerness and who hold space for queers who are struggling for any reason. Queerness is for loving and being loved—but I mean that in the most woo, community, and world-minded way possible and *not* simply interpersonally. When I say being who we are regardless is an act of queer liberation, I promise I want you to take your safety into account too. Sometimes it's not safe where we live or work, and rolling our eyes at a homophobic joke or chiding our uncle's casual transphobia is the most we can do. Sometimes making and holding space for others is all we can do. Sometimes admitting we need space someone else held or made is all we are capable of. That is enough. I promise.

Welcome!

About the Essayists

I want to introduce you to our incredible essayists right off the bat. I am so unbelievably honored and touched that these nine people agreed to write essays with me for this collection. They were all absolute angels to work with, and I am ecstatic at what we've put together. Bios are in an appendix at the back of this book, but I wanted to ease you into this essay collection by gushing about how much I love these nine people. This list is in alphabetical order because no way in heck was I going to attempt to rank them in some way.

Maria the Arcane is one of the sweetest people I have ever met in my life, which I learned when she interviewed me as part of the *Coffee & Cauldrons* podcast hosting team (the other host being writer Robyn Valentine who is also warm and wonderful) for the *Lessons from the Empress* book release. In addition to being a sweetheart, she won me over completely by her gorgeous photos of her own craft on Instagram. She digs deep with her cohosting spot on *Coffee & Cauldrons*, and her essay featured here on discovering her sexuality through the gentleness of the Empress brought me to tears.

Charlie Claire Burgess and I have long shared digital spaces. We also share an agent, which is how I ended up writing the forward for their debut book *Radical Tarot*, which is so good, so of the moment, and so freaking smart that I wish I'd written it. I've been so honored when we've been on panels or in meetings together. Now I'm extra honored to share these pages with them. Charlie went all in on a brilliant piece about Court Cards as interstitial elements. Months after receiving this piece, it still blows my mind.

Asali Earthwork is an absolute dream of a friend and has been ever since way back in our Little Red Tarot days. She's someone whose work in the blogosphere and on social media is unparalleled in driving the community of witchy queers forward. I've mentioned her Tarot of the QTPOC already, but her unique style when interviewing deck creators makes for some of my favorite posts of hers too. In this collection, she bravely takes us on a tour of her own grief as she goes through the Major Arcana from a state of it.

Maria Minnis is, IMQO, the future of tarot, and I said as much when I blurbed her debut, *Tarot for the Hard Work*. The fact that her writing is so perfectly offbeat in this collection cannot disguise how wicked smart she is (I don't think anything could!) and only serves to tie together ideas someone else would never be able to. Specifically, Maria's inclusion in this book welcomes us to a community of lichen. She shows us how communities of lichen mirror the idealized sense of community in the suit of Cups and how that mirrors so much of the work so many of us queer humans are trying to do.

Junauda Petrus and I have been circling around each other where we live for a long time. I had the absolute bliss of seeing her read from her YA (young adult) novel *The Stars and the Blackness Between Them* (which peppers in stunning astrology poems throughout) at a local author event. Her essay "The High Priestess as Black Femme Memory" is one of my favorite things I have ever read, and I am so unbelievably honored to be including it here.

Siri Vincent Plouff is notoriously one of my best friends IRL (in real life)—and I do say this intentionally as we are known chaos monsters together in our social circle. We became friends because I was moved by some early blogging they were doing about discovering self on a progressive Heathen path. Their writing continues to move me whether they are writing about fighting anti-racism in Heathenry or queering how we think of tarot reversals, the latter of which they are doing in this anthology. Siri and I coauthored *Lessons from the Empress* together, and I am so thrilled to still be in cahoots with them now, especially for the incredibly thought-provoking essay they penned here, "Trick Mirror Tarot."

Rebecca Scolnick is a perfect example of how this world *needs* everyone in this collection. She is constantly showing up for so many of us as a friend and colleague in the most genuine way. I do not want her kindness to overshadow her work though. Her writing on numerology online and her debut book, *The Witch's Book of Numbers*, has completely changed how I practice tarot, occultism, and witchcraft. She is as brilliant as she is lovable, and that is very much! You'll fall in love with her too as she recounts her own journey to queerness and what certain cards, including a couple Minor Arcana that often get overlooked, mean to her in that journey.

Taylor Ursula I met through teaching for a yearlong course by Corinna Rosella of the *Rise Up! Good Witch* podcast. Her tarot insights combined with the way she seamlessly weaves some serious astrology knowledge through them is like nothing I've quite seen before (in all the best ways). Here, she's provided us with an essay on how she developed those methods and what queering symbolism as a whole means to her. I originally asked for "something about astrology in the tarot" and got a piece completely reinventing how and why we process symbology entirely. Plus, you get a sneak peek of their wonderful Portals tarot deck!

Meg Jones Wall and I officially met in a writer's group but had been friendly online for quite a while before that. Their inaugural book, *Finding the Fool*, beautifully breaks down tarot cards by sensory experience, astrological meaning, and modern-day takes on traditional numerology. I knew when I read that book that I just had to include something by them for *Tarot in Other Words*. Their piece on queer numbers became an absolute cornerstone for this book, and I cannot wait for you to read it.

These essayists and I come together to drive home one of my most formative beliefs in queerness as orientation to friendship and community as well as the romantic, gendered, or sexual. What we hope to offer here are ten different points of view on what the cards can mean for us as queer folk. We hope we give you plenty of information, insight, and interpretation to further your journey. We hope we write in a way that makes you feel welcomed to these conversations instead of talked at. We hope, simply put, that you are finding your way through the world the best way you can, armed with a deck of tarot cards to guide you. We're beside ourselves that you would consider our words part of that journey too.

PART I

FINDING OURSELVES IN THE TAROT

Introduction

When people started turning in essays for this collection, it became very clear that those essays fell into one of two camps: personal storytelling that highlights the powerful ways tarot can move through and transform us and instructional materials highlighting techniques and opportunities for you to look at tarot in new and queer-inclusive ways. That's not to say there's not overlap—there definitely is. Even that attempt at classification and noticing the overlap plays with the themes of fluidity, being, and what we owe to each other that are so important in both queer and radical theory.

This overlap illustrates another thing I really love about queer writing and storytelling too: the way we, as queers, are able to utilize how the specific, in spite of how hyperpersonal and vulnerable it can feel to share, is somehow even more relatable. That goes all the way back to why we tell stories and share information in the first place. We tell our own stories no matter what. We do it because telling these stories is rebellion. It is preservation. It is connection. It helps build relationships, maintain an oral and written history, and find each other. Some of the storytelling pieces in this collection are, at times, academic or logical in nature too. They are technical, focused on tarot method. They are also still gorgeous examples of queer story. They also exhibit the way tarot itself can be rooted in storytelling of past, present, and future. We as people—especially as queer people—are multifaceted. Because of the very nature of our genders and sexualities (not to mention the occasional need for code-switching), we are wonderful at embracing all of the both/and/beyonds within ourselves. We are masters of technique and skill, *and* we are inspired storytellers. We are full of innovative ideas; we call on long histories of queer lineages, *and* we have things close to our own hearts that we want to share.

Nonetheless, this book felt easiest and best when broken into two sections. Here in Part 1, "Finding Ourselves in the Tarot," we look at, essentially, why tarot matters. These are stories of times we were struggling or overjoyous and looking for that everywhere. We wanted spiritual connection to it. We wanted to be seen by the gods. We wanted to be seen in our own mirrors, which tarot is often compared to. Finding yourself in the tarot is something that most white, able-bodied, cisgender, and heterosexual people take for granted. They crack open a tarot deck or book, and everyone looks like them. Everyone is presumed to share their experience and presumed to be headed toward similar goals. It's assumed that the deck creator or book writer is coming from a similar framework and point of view as them. Queer people, BIPOC (Black, indigenous, people of color), those of us who are disabled—we have never been able to take that for granted. We have always done one of two things: searched for ourselves or created something totally new.

The writers in this section have done a little bit of both of these things, and it is a freaking delight. They have searched for themselves in the tarot, and they have come up with brand new memories, images, and ideas that place themselves amongst the tarot cards. They do so in a lovely, expansive way that will not only *allow* you to do the same thing but *inspire* you to do so. These Part 1 writers have also, at times, simply created new structures and understandings of the tarot cards for themselves.

It is so easy for people to leave tarot in the 1400s, the 1900s, or wherever they see it as originating. These essays shows that tarot is a breathing, evolving structure that absolutely can grow with us. Nothing in this book is meant to be set in stone. We only want queer people and their stories to have the place we deserve in tarot canon. I hope you do not read through this section and feel as though you have to memorize all new concepts and keywords. Instead, I hope you are able to read this section, go through your own deck, and get similarly creative.

And . . .

I hope you read these essays, shuffle through your deck, and see yourself in ways and places you never expected to.

With that, let's jump in!

THE GRIEVING FOOL

by Asali Earthwork

Queerness is expansive, as it should be. There is very little that can be said to be fundamental to each queer person's individual experience. What is one thing I can say that every queer person has felt or experienced—other than the very reality of being queer? I sat with this question when Cassandra invited me to be a part of this anthology as I brainstormed where to land, what to write, and how to connect. Is it love? Perhaps. So much of what we tie to queerness is a reference to who we love, how we love . . . but that sadly cannot always be a sure thing. It isn't a milestone we will all experience.

Rather morbidly, instead of love, I settled on grief. If there is an experience that we the here and queer have all experienced, at least once (though most likely never so singularly), it is grief. Grief for self, community, possibility, futures, and so much more. Grief is not all we have. We've had entire oceans of love, hope, community, pleasure, inspiration, and dreams of beautiful queer futures.[1] I can taste these oceans in the salt of the tears shed when the grief makes itself known anew, every

---

[1] I will return to water often in my engagement with grief work; water is memory, liminality, Black and queer history, medicine, gravekeeper, and so much more than can be articulated—as with grief itself. I thank Yemaya, Oshun, Alexis Pauline Gumbs (2018, 2020), M. Jacqui Alexander (2005), Lucille Clifton (2020), Sharon Bridgforth (2004), and Audre Lorde (2000) for their lessons in the language of water that nourished me in my own grieving.

time. I claim it as a celebration of the capacity of our love; so to say that to be queer is to know grief is no condemnation.

Grief is no standalone feeling. I've met it as a journey[2]—one with no clear destination but one that winds and returns and sets off again. If we're talking tarot and queerness,[3] that feels very familiar in the context of the Fool's Journey. What if we approached grief in the context of the Fool's Journey? If we are the Grieving Fool, and the cliff that we walk off is grief, how does that shift the familiar tarot path? How does it create new paths or even obstacles? I come to the cards of the Major Arcana as signposts that we might orient ourselves around as we journey through our grief. Sometimes there is medicine and guidance, and some cards are simply there as mirror or witness. I invite you to fall off the cliff of this experiment with me. Of course, as with all tarot interpretations, your own intuition and understanding should lead you. There is no one understanding of any tarot card or of queerness. There is also no one experience of grief.

0. The Fool

The shock of it.

The loss of breath.

A stuttering heartbeat.

Space—suddenly too much space where there was once who or what we just lost.

We are lost without a clear way forward, not even come to terms with the actual loss. The ground has moved and is no longer beneath us. If you should pull the Fool in your grief journey, know that action is the last thing being asked of you. the Fool is surrender, and we are asked to fully surrender to the grief, let it lead us where it may. That is its own kind of medicine, allowing ourselves to fully sink in the

---

[2] I write a series on grief work on my blog called *Grief Journeys*.
[3] You should absolutely have *Queering the Tarot* by Cassandra Snow (2019) in your library.

saltwater and let the waves crash over us. It cannot be said enough that this will hurt, be deeply uncomfortable and overwhelming—and it is meant to be. We can hold on to that one certainty as the grief current carries us where it will. It is here that we are connected to the portal of love that grief creates, and even as we shatter, we are breaking into something new. I can promise you that there is an us that will eventually wash up on shore.

1. The Magician

Can The Reaper come to us as the Magician? I say yes. Even if we are not yet ready to take them up, there are resources and tools available to us in the grieving work. What are your tried-and-true methods of comfort, healing, and soothing when the hurt is cutting deepest? Perhaps you are being asked to turn to what is already within you or available to you. Lack and loss often inspire the indomitable spirit, and we surprise ourselves with our capacity to keep carrying on. Because the Magician is also a trickster, remember to look where you might not first think to seek. What shapes itself as loss can transform into a portal we can dive into to find something new. Look to our queer histories for examples and you will find an abundance of examples of us turning the loss of safety, family, and opportunity into resistance, dance, and new ways to connect to each other. We can carry on, shining even brighter. If we give grief its space, we'll find that *we* were the Magician after all.

2. The High Priestess

Before we can effectively harness the Magician's tools, we need to be still and listen deeply. Here in the High Priestess, you make space for the grief to become an avenue of communication—not just with who we might have lost, but with our deeper selves. In the deep quiet dark, the waves of grief muffling all external sound, we can hear the messages that need to be heard. This time is necessary, and if you pull the High Priestess in your grieving journey, it may be an invitation to draw away for some time and spend some in the stillness. There are sacred secrets that we can only find in the grieving journey, and we won't hear them in the hustle of what the world considers the work of *moving on*.

3. The Empress

One of my favorite reimaginings of the Empress card is in the *Slow Holler Tarot*'s renaming to the Kindred.[4] In this card we are invited to remember that grieving is not a solo project. While there is time for quiet and individual introspection, grief work is also collective. Not only for the fact that there can no longer be an experience of grief that we are the very first to feel, it is also imperative that we allow ourselves to be reached for and held. We can turn to our chosen families, community connections, and the very earth itself to find a place to be supported and ground into. Moreover, the Empress pulls us away from the instinct to succumb to numbness as an escape route and asks us to allow ourselves to feel even deeper—engage the senses in our grief and also in how we find comfort. The Empress as the Kindred also allows us to share the load, as there is pain no one mortal body is meant to carry alone.[5] On an absolutely practical level, grief lives in the body and taxes it, and so we must remember to prioritize physical nourishment. We need to eat well and drink plenty of water. Often that's as much as we can do on days when the grief is laying on us heaviest, and that is its own kind of plenty.

---

[4] The *Slow Holler Tarot* (2016) is an exceptional deck with radical reinterpretations of The Major Arcana, the Kindred being just one. Unfortunately, it is out of print, but if you've had the opportunity to snag a copy, it is one of my absolute recommendations in terms of decks that are excellent for grief work.

[5] Grief work, calling us back to our trauma and loss, can often expose us to a pain, and sometimes it is necessarily "one that is held not by an individual but by the collective and mediated by the divine so that it does not overwhelm the mortal body," as Matt Richardson (2013, 99) notes in his rich examination of *love conjure/blues* by Sharon Bridgforth.

4. The Emperor

Can grief provide structure? Is safety even possible? Or does it all come apart—at times necessarily? These are the two questions that came up for me when facing the Emperor in the context of grief. After all, grief is often a result of the dissolution of a structure or safety we relied upon, as represented by the person, place, thing, or idea we have lost. Consider that often what we try to do is fill that space. We seek something or someone else to fill up that space for us without much consideration from one to the next. We grow hard edges, firm up, and seek to protect ourselves from further hurt by drawing our defenses up higher, thicker, tougher. That can be necessary, for a time, but it is *not* sustainable. The Emperor's energy is not sustainable without the Empress's balance. We need the Kindred, we need softness, we need support, we simply *need*.

The Emperor can also be the cause of grief, not just how we embody our response to grieving. We see this play on a daily basis with engines of imperialism and colonialism causing immeasurable violence and grief to occur in service to their necropolitical goals. Our grief work must turn collective in order to transform it into righteous rage and justice work. It reminds us of our humanity and connection to each other, and so we must harness it into speech and action in service of the new world we must urgently create where we live in reciprocity. This is the grief work that reminds us that there is an Emperor energy that can provide safety—not suffocation.

5. The Hierophant

The Hierophant's marker on the path of grief work is a reminder that we are not alone. Not only can the person we've lost still be with us, but we are also not the first to grieve, and there is a well of grieving knowledge as deep as the oceans to draw from. For some of us, especially us queer folks, those archives of grief become the community that holds us until we find (and I hold a prayer that we all may find) our community in the present. We add to the archive when we share our grief work, both the questions and the insights, with ourselves and others. The Hierophant is a reminder that those tear-stained pages in your journal may be a balm to you in a later grief; that art submission to a grief zine may give some stranger back the knowledge to breathe and keep breathing through the pain. A queer Hierophant also knows that the traditional archive is not all there is—we can leave our wisdom in gardens of rosemary, bricks of resistance, gumbo recipes, and acts of compassion just as well as we can write them down to be stored away.

6. The Lovers

Grief reveals the weight of our love. Isn't that quite the gift? When you work with the Lovers in grief work, allow it to remind you of your capacity for care, compassion, and empathy. Let it invite you toward more softness, more connection, more depth of feeling. It asks us to rely on the lessons of the previous cards, which showed that the weight of what is shared does not bog down. Even as the enormity of hurt, trauma, loss pervades our bodies and spirits, it is in those tendrils of connection that ease and comfort are found. Reach out to each other, reach out to all of your selves—inner child and future ancestor. Reach out (back) into the moon and earth; find the mirror that relieves the load in the light of reflection.[6] Grief work is a love practice.

7. The Chariot

You might be tempted to look at the Chariot in a reading on grief and feel that you are being asked to move forward, take charge, and

---

[6] My favorite Lovers card is found in the *Next World Tarot* by Cristy C. Road (2018). It depicts a disabled, fat, femme of color looking into the mirror at their own reflection with love and witness (Road). The whole deck is top tier, and it is still available!

find a new direction. While I won't discount that possibility entirely, I wonder if we are falling into the Chariot's own trap—caught up in the external shine of armor and chaos of charging on without looking inward for what actually makes the whole thing—chariot, reined horses, armored rider, all go forward. The Chariot's astrological correspondence is the sign of Cancer—a sign associated deeply with water, sensitivity, intuition, and empathy. It is this that draws us away from just plain moving onward and forward and asks us to consider what is in our hearts. How can you let your heart take the lead in this grief work? How can you let that be the center of gravity that roots you to the floor of the Chariot and drive you forward with more stability? How might that change what steps you take on the grief journey?

8. Strength

First, there is the obvious interpretation of Strength. Here we learn that we are capable of handling this too, that we can survive and find a way forward even with this pain, that we have the capacity and the will to keep going even if the effort seems like too much most days. Also, Strength is the understanding that we do not subdue the lion of grief by bending it to our will. Instead, we meet it with compassion and realize that we are meeting ourselves. Strength in the grief journey is a signpost asking us to reject the urge to control and force ourselves into healing that we are simply not ready for. The medicine is in the tenderness and that in every one of our wailing roars we are purging poison, so please practice compassion with self and others. Compassion is a reminder that our resilience will not be found in the refusal to feel. Yes, grief is a trial by fire, but one that must be tended to, not just snuffed out or allowed to scorch the earth.

9. The Hermit

The Hermit takes the time to pull back, leave the noise, and go to the quiet to find their center again. We need Kindred, and sometimes we need time with ourselves. In the Grieving Fool's Journey, the Hermit's sign is a waystation or, at times, a detour toward the darkness and stillness of the cave. A place where we are able to take some time to reflect and appraise our journey so far. What are the truths that have revealed themselves in your grief work? Are we allowing ourselves ample time to grapple with them and let them decide the path of the grief journey? This time alone can be both deeply soothing and wildly uncomfortable depending on where we are in our grief work. There is no right feeling except what we are feeling in the moment. The Hermit also reminds us that we are not meant to be alone and in the dark for all time; they do carry a lamp after all. It is both a source of light for them and for our Kindred to more easily find us should we get too lost in the darkness.

10. The Wheel of Fortune

The Wheel of Fortune reiterates the limits of control and exposes where we might be holding tightly to what is actually nothing at all. It is not just understanding that we are constantly in the "wheel of time" and so in natural cycles of life and death; it is also allowing ourselves to be surprised by what comes from grief work. You might be surprised with what you learn after some time with the Hermit's energy. One of the most fascinating aspects of grief is how genuinely surprising it can be—and not always unpleasantly. As an example, I was surprised with how much relief came at the heels of losing my mother. To be clear, I am still absolutely devastated, but I am also relieved by the possibilities of new ways to connect, to hear and be heard beyond the limitations of this physical world. I have come to know her and be connected to her with so much more grace than either of us were capable of when we both were in our physical bodies. Incredibly, the love grew even deeper, and forgiveness was more possible for hurts that seemed like mountains before her passing on. This has been just one of the surprises. What are new ways of knowing and loving that have been revealed to you in your grief work? How have you engaged with the inevitability of change that is both an action and a reaction of grief?

11. Justice

Sometimes what we grieve is not a result of a natural ending. Sometimes it is abrupt and brought on by a lack of justice. In our grief we can find the strength to rage, to hold accountable, and to choose to do better. Justice is Adjustment in the *Thoth Tarot* tradition. In the context of grief, I meet it as the way we make space for the different forms of us that are created in grief, understanding that there is no one way forward—as long as we are truthful in how we choose to move forward, allowing for the space of that movement and adjusting to the needs of ourselves and our communities' needs and meeting ourselves as we are. In a reading on grief, it may be a moment to take account of and be accountable to how you have treated yourself and others as you moved through your grief journey. What are the consequences of those choices made? In this way it reminds us of agency we too easily forget in the onslaught of all that we feel when we grieve. Again, I return to my initial reading of this card. In the face of injustice that actively generates loss, trauma, and death, what are the choices we can make? What actions can be different and better? Small or imperfect, there is always something.[7]

---

7   I love how Charlie puts it in their Justice section in *Radical Tarot*: "An unceasing process of change, adjustment, and adaptability . . . what Justice does require is *action*. It requires *trying*" (Burgess 2023, 100).

12. The Hanged One

Surrender again. Again? Yes, again.

There is no scheduling grief. It will arrive how it arrives in all the ways you expect and don't expect whether the loss is fresh as minutes ago or decades past. Each time it asks us to feel, with depth and authenticity, all of the wave from trough to crest. The external world tends to rush grief processes and becomes indignant that those of us with loss still seem to carry it fresh days, weeks, years, centuries, entire generations later. It then dares to shame and dismiss us for holding ourselves tenderly still. I say *that* is the absurdity—not us turned upside down in open and inviting surrender to our grief letting it be what it will.

13. Death

Death is sometimes just that, death. So I'll start there. In a reading on grief, pulling this card may be a check-in moment. Have we come to terms with our loss? Have we fully accepted—and I mean *fully*—what it is we have lost and the possible scope of that loss? Are we moving too fast to the next steps in the journey before sitting with the reality? Maybe a part of us is still in denial, bargaining . . . you know the rest. Whichever stage you're in, that's okay. It's just important to be truthful with ourselves about it. Let it be messy, painful, jagged, and ugly. From facing the realities of loss, we can then safely and wholly move forward into the other possibilities this card opens us up to. Death is also what leads to rebirth and transformation. Nature, our greatest and wisest teacher, shares this lesson on a daily basis. In this uncomfortable and painful grief work is the necessary alchemy that leads to transformation.

14. Temperance

I love pulling this card in grief work, and it is because of that that I feel unable to fully articulate all that it can be. I offer no absolutes in how to read this card. Bear with me. The reason is that Temperance is so much like grieving—doing its work in the liminal space, neither here nor there, starting and ending just to begin again, at the meeting of worlds, defying expectations and feeling just as we expect it to sometimes. Temperance walks with Death, and so I say again that grief is a practice of alchemy. We tap into the mysteries to transform ourselves into something completely new—an us without (without that or them that we lost) and with so much more because of it. It is impossible to contain in time and space, and so it gives us permission to be formless in our grief when needed and knit ourselves back together when we are ready and unravel all over again. We can neither lie prone and completely destroyed by the weight of loss, nor can we sustain the hard-edged stoicism of refusing to feel the loss. We spiral, coming back again and again but never the same each time.

15. The Devil

There are traps in the grief journey—pits we fall into that leave us with the false certainty that despair is all there is or that moving forward requires us to bury the pain deep and never let it out again. Either way, we are trapped, and we certainly aren't doing the work of grief anymore. The Devil is not the pause or darkness of the High Priestess, the Hermit, or the Hanged One. This is stuck energy, stagnation, suppression, and deoxygenation. Very practically, the Devil also addresses our coping strategies—remember those tried and true? I used the word *true* intentionally, because sometimes what we turn to in order to cope provides no true balm or healing and we must get real about that before it leaves us worse off. The Devil asks us to address the limits of how we choose to cope. It is not about shaming ourselves for turning to those strategies—we did so because they did *something*—but to acknowledge that different choices must be made.

In the collective context, the Devil can also be about the true evils that cause unnecessary and unnatural loss outside of the natural cycle of our world. The grief of oppression is immeasurable and daunting—or at least it seems that way for those of us living with privilege. The Devil is the reminder that even on these larger scales with so much at stake, we still have responsibility. It asks the difficult questions. Where are we complicit and participant? What chains can be broken to free all of us? What more will we have to be willing to lose for it? Where have we given up and said it's all too much and chosen inaction? Those facing the violence of oppression are often the ones dreaming up the most radical dreams of freedom and an apocalypse that destroys the old empire and rings in a world of equity. Trans and queer people created Pride; Black dreamers conceived Afrofuturism; to this day Palestinian elders keep the original keys to the homes they were violently ejected from. So really, how can those of us with any privilege lose hope and give into despair? Let the grief radicalize you instead and grant you unflinching hope.

16. The Tower

The Tower's energy comes to shake the ground and break it open with a bolt of lightning so powerful it went through all that was above the ground and still had enough electricity left to take that apart too. As with other cards we've met so far, there is more than one way the Tower card can show up in the reading. Sometimes it shows up as a representation of all the ways we have chosen to protect ourselves from the full depth of our grief, walling ourselves as thickly and highly as possible so that the waves of grief will not reach us.[8] This card laughs in the face of that and exposes it for the false protection it is. That kind of tower is doomed to come down. Things fall apart. The Tower can also represent the ways in which loss landed in our lives. With little warning and in the space of a second, we are left with nothing but rubble to pick through. Here is where the grief work begins. Our hands will break open on the stones as we try to salvage what we can so we can start again somehow. Remember that salvage is not always possible or the best way forward. Part of the grief work is also recognizing what shit needs to be left in the rubble so that Earth, so much wiser and craftier than us, can regenerate it into something new and nourishing.

17. The Star

The kindness of the Star can be the most difficult medicine to swallow when in the throes of grief. How dare a reminder of hope and healing show up in the face of the loss? And yet it does, and it is available to us at all times for when we are ready to dare to take up its cup and let the healing water pour over us. It is not disrespectful to who or what we lost for the pain to ease, for the weight to lighten, or to relearn breathing one stuttering shallow inhale at a time. It should then not cut off our access to hope even when the pain rolls over tenfold, the weight is heavier, and breathing easy is suddenly a difficult-to-reach memory. The Star is the possibility that we will one day feel "better," and that is okay. *The Star is also the possibility that we will have to find a new definition of "better" and that is okay too.* As we do our grief work, let us remain open to possibilities as numerous as the very stars themselves, as infinite as the universe they are suspended in.

---

8 Gumbs (2018) asks, "do you know what it feels like to love a wall with all your waking days and dreaming nights? you will do anything to keep it" (144).

18. The Moon

In the darkness of grief work, closer than the light of the stars is that of the Moon. If you've ever tried to find your way around outside with nothing but its light, you know to be grateful for its light and discerning about the edges of the shapes it creates. The Moon in a reading about grief asks us to look beyond what is right in front of us; it is a searching that is internal and teaches us to discern between what is truth and what is simply illusion. As much as grief can sharpen our focus and shine on what is truly important, it can also cause a lack of clarity. The Moon as signpost in the grief journey asks us to be even more attentive to the internal self. It's often a sign we've been looking everywhere else for answers when we already had them within us the whole time.

The Moon is also deeply associated with the depth of our feeling. In a reading it asks us to go within, sink into ourselves with even more intention and, most importantly, with deeper trust. It is a radical thing to trust yourself when you have been laid low by trauma. It's a soft challenge to go further in the work of grief work and have faith that you will come out on the other side. Perhaps what we believe is lost is just waiting to be found in a new form within ourselves. The hard work of living in this world can create in us layers of grief, and it takes time and intention to excavate them. Whatever is unburied, have faith in the truth of the grief work you are doing and turn to the resources you have accumulated so far as the Grieving Fool.

19. The Sun

The Sun challenges us to allow for the possibility of its existence even within grief. I will not promise that everything will be okay—doing so would be disingenuous at best. However, as we move through grief work, we are working to unbury in tandem with the burying. The Sun highlights what has come through and provides the sharper focus we have earned in doing the work of listening quietly, seeking out, and facing difficult truths. Unlike the soft light of the Moon, the Sun has the intensity to illuminate all uncovered corners and leave us bare. Exposure isn't always comfortable, especially when loss and trauma mean we can see what was missing so much clearer—all that never-found closure that was withheld and feels so far beyond us is now in another realm. Often what is revealed is even more grief work to be done. What we can do in the face of this light is know that even in this is opportunity for growth and understanding. We are capable of so much more when we aren't doing everything we can to look away from the messy and uncomfortable realities.

The Sun invites the grief outward as a reclamation of power—let the world face what it has wrought on us. It would be much easier for this violent world and those responsible for it if we all hid away our trauma and just got along. Let the horrors committed in the dark be borne out in the sunlight. These are the first steps of demanding accountability. On the very simplest and most personal level, outwardly grieving allows Kindred even closer so they may offer needed care and succor.

20. Judgement

Then one day, we find we have more space in our lungs to breathe—that the very first breathing was done underwater, so we only returned to the birth of everything while grappling with death.[9] As lovely as a scene of the heavens parting and the multitudes rejoicing might be, I prefer the reality of acknowledging what it took to break the surface. You have traveled far, dearest Fool, and it has been no smooth journey. Take a moment to locate and hold up joy in the victory of having

---

9   Referencing the "cradle of life" as the oceans, "she taught them about breathing and that the first way to do it is underwater . . . and she would continue to teach them so many things, simply by being alive" (Gumbs 2018, 209).

made it just a few more steps forward with all the authenticity you could bring to this work. It is a wonder every moment we keep going; you are a wonder. Remember gratitude for yourself, Kindred, and the Divine that is always with you. Relish the new connections to what you carried forward from the loss and the new ways you have reassembled yourself in the aftermath. There is yet more to do, and you will rejoice after that work too.

21. The World

The World is all that is possible and the wholeness of the journey. The World is all of the signposts of each card so far. The World is how we can bring what we have found within us to the external world and share our new possibilities, radical worlds that seemed so far beyond us. The World is these multitudes, and the World is also who and what was lost and is being tended to and grieved—for we know that each life is a whole world . So more often than not, we begin the journey again and take the path of the Grieving Fool. Of course, much like the much-discussed "stages of grief," there is no guarantee you will meet each of the Arcana in numerical order. Grief is nonlinear, so you will come to each of these signposts at different times as the waves carry you. Spend as much time as you need to wherever you need to, however many times you need to. The work of grief is the work of lifetimes.

Tarot Spread for Checking in with Grief Work[10]

1. BREAK OPEN
2. CRASHING WAVE
3. GASP OF BREATH
4. OPEN SURRENDER
5. BREAK THROUGH

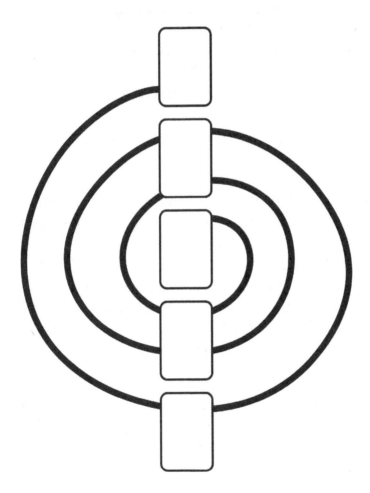

---

10 I share an example of a reading I did with this spread on the first anniversary of my mother's passing (Asali, 2015–2018). The spaces for the cards are intentionally unnumbered and the orientation can be shifted vertically or horizontally so that you decide which direction to set your cards in.

THE GRIEVING FOOL

Citation as Sacred Practice

Alexander, M. Jacqui. *Pedagogies of Crossing: Meditations on Feminism, Sexual Politics, Memory, and the Sacred.* Duke University Press, 2005.

Asali. *Grief Journeys.* 2015–2018. asaliearthwork.com.

Bridgforth, Sharon. *love conjure/blues.* RedBone Press, 2004.

Burgess, Charlie Claire. *Radical Tarot: Queer the Cards, Liberate Your Practice, and Create the Future.* Hay House, 2023.

Clifton, Lucille. *How to Carry Water: Selected Poems.* Ed. Aracelis Girmay. BOA Editions Ltd., 2020.

Gumbs, Alexis Pauline. *M Archive: After the End of the World.* Duke University Press, 2018.

—. *Undrowned: Black Feminist Lessons from Marine Mammals.* AK Press, 2020.

Lorde, Audre. *The Collected Poems of Audre Lorde.* Norton, 2000.

Richardson, Matt. *The Queer Limit of Black Memory: Black Lesbian Literature and Irresolution.* The Ohio State University Press, 2013.

Road, Cristy C. *Next World Tarot.* Silver Sprocket, 2018.

Slow Holler. *Slow Holler Tarot.* 2016.

Snow, Cassandra. *Queering the Tarot.* Weiser Books, 2019.

Tinsley, Omise'eke Natasha. "Black Atlantic, Queer Atlantic: Queer Imaginings of the Middle Passage." *GLQ: A Journal of Lesbian and Gay Studies* 14 (2008): 191–215.

QUEERNESS HAS NO TIMELINE

Exploring a Slower Journey with the Magician, the Four of Wands, and the Seven of Pentacles

By Rebecca Scolnick

The first person I came out to was Tinder. Not my mom, not my best friend, but the endless flipbook of faces that made up my local, online, singles pool.

I'd had success on the app before (if you can call hooking up with a well-endowed neighbor after he'd roped me into paying for both of our beers or getting ghosted by a Comedy Central writer who loved both e e cummings and lying as favorable results), and as it began to sink in that my attractions and desires weren't as singular as my church upbringing had led me to believe, it seemed like a safe space to flex my newfound interests. A sensation of delightful blasphemy ran through my body as I ticked the virtual box, switching my feed to show *both men and women*.

I was twenty-two, and the world had suddenly opened up before me.

There had been signs that foreshadowed my future as a queer person: the pair of Doc Martens I swiped from a community theatre production of *Rent*, the picture of Helen Mirren in a red bikini wallpapering my phone, the hours spent under the covers in my childhood bedroom watching **gasp** uncensored YouTube compilations of *Queer as Folk*'s Brian and Justin reclaiming their right to dance in public to ABBA's "Chiquitita," among other more naughty things. Not to mention the nights spent cuddling with someone who was "just a friend," both before and after they came out as transgender. There were miraculous markers that shined like beacons as I looked backward to validate that I was on the correct road—evidence to support that I'd come to the right conclusion. There was also *grief*. Doubt. Shame and uncertainty over the years I'd spent in ignorance of myself.

How could I not have *known*? Shouldn't I have answered these questions earlier? Don't most people know sooner? (The median age that most queer folks know is seventeen.[11]) I've always supported and celebrated my siblings in the LGBTQIA+ community, but how could I have spent so long not knowing to count myself among them?

Was I even queer enough to be queer?

I've come to realize queerness has no timeline. There is no rule that says that you must know at seventeen, twenty-two, thirty-five, or eighty-seven. There isn't an age that one hits that bars them from learning, or accepting, or changing, or questioning. There is no such thing as *too early*, and there is no such thing as *too late*. Life is an endless cycle of moments and experiences through which we can come into deeper connection and intimacy with our ever-changing selves. Regardless of what other voices and systems of programming may say, there is no empirical evidence to support the idea that it would even be possible for us to stay the same, day after day, for an entire lifetime. Our bodies are an ecosystem of bacteria, genetic materials, and star stuff. Our cells die and are reborn every moment. The one who wakes up is not the one who goes to bed next.

---

11   Pew Research Center, *Chapter 3: The Coming Out Experience*, "A Survey of LGBT Americans," Pew Research Center's Social & Demographic Trends Project, June 13, 2013, pewresearch.org.

Change is natural. It's promised. It is God.[12] Change is also scary. It rattles our bones and churns in our guts. It can throw off our entire system if fear really gets its hooks in. That fear can become intertwined with who we think we are and what we think we need, want, love, and value. That fear is also easily exploited. It's targeted and spoken to. Stoked. Amplified. Used to keep us from seeing eye-to-eye (or heart-to-heart), locked in cycles of oppression and bondage. Most importantly, that fear keeps us from ourselves. It keeps us from feeling powerful, trustworthy, and deserving. Blocks us from our true creative, cyclical, gnostic nature. Because empowered change? Intentional change? *Embodied* change? That's downright dangerous.

Thankfully, if you're reading this right now, you probably like a little risk.

That, or you need a little push. A little tender love, and *come on babe, you can do it!* from a friend who's been there before. Maybe you've been there before too, but some of it still stings in the rearview. Perhaps the inklings have been there all along, and while the clock isn't ticking, the time has come. For all I know you're staring down the barrel of another change, another identity, another self. Wherever you are, you're right on time. Come on in, have a seat. There is no wrong time to remeet yourself. You're in good company too, for no one really knows much about anything. You have allies along the way.

Which brings us to our mutual friend, the tarot.

A deck of tarot cards offers seventy-eight mirrors of wisdom, guidance, and *maitri* for you to hold in your hands and call upon whenever you find yourself at a crossroads of your past, present, and future selves, whether it's for the first time or the thousandth time.[13] The tarot can be an incredible tool for self-reflection and self-knowledge and can provide

---

12   O. E. Butler, *Parable of the Sower* (Grand Central Publishing, 2019).
13   "Pema Chödrön: Explaining Maitri," FindCenter, *findcenter.com*.

a nuanced and flexible system of support when it comes to exploring concepts as complex as sexuality, especially if you're driving a gentler, meandering, scenic route in the slow lane. The tarot can also be a magical mapmaker that provides what Dame Helen gave to me: enough certainty and belonging to keep going.

It can be as hard to move forward in darkness as it is to swallow a whole new reality, so I asked the tarot to narrow it down, and the three cards that stepped forward as guides for us slow burners and late bloomers were **the Magician**, the **Four of Wands**, and the **Seven of Pentacles**.

While at first glance these cards seem to hold very different fractals of experience, they are all numerologically connected. One (the Magician), four, and seven are the three numbers that represent the *practical* energies of numerology's building block numbers of one through nine. They represent a grounded and Earth-bound approach, touching on themes of trust, effort, exploration, growth, perseverance, and much, much more. It makes total sense why they'd show up for us now—pragmatism and matter-of-factness are lovely copilots along a perilous path like queerness. They'll help us to ensure that the time spent wading through our thoughts and emotions can also be put into action and made manifest in our lives. Practicality ensures that rubber meets the road.

Let's ride.

The Magician

The second card of the Major Arcana, the Magician, stands majestically with the number one, conjuring themes of the self, the start and the esoteric principle, *as above, so below*.

Look closely, and you'll come to understand the trickster spirit that lies within the tarot's second card, but also the first. What you see isn't always what you get. Were you watching carefully enough to catch the Magician's sleight of hand? Cloaked in white, and with a fierce clarity of purpose and direction, the Magician alchemizes self and Spirit to perform marvels and miracles. Who's to say what's real or an illusion? Perception creates reality. While the fire blazed, it lived and breathed, didn't it? The Magician is of both Earth and Sky. Here and There. In this world, yet not of it.

Sounds queer to me.

Within this delicious doubling is also a portal back to yourself, or a way through to your new self. The occultic aphorism "know thyself" has a long history of varied uses, but at its core lies the sentiment that self-knowledge is the key to connecting our values, will, and actions. If we understand *why* we feel, act, and react in certain ways, we can open ourselves up to other possibilities. But how do we engage with the process of learning about ourselves, especially when the self that's showing up seems foreign or unexpected? If your queerness has come as a surprise lightning strike in the storm, you may be dealing with a sense of self that relates to the oft-forgotten charlatan aspects of the Magician, which can be hard to connect with or to trust.

Luckily, we're still at the beginning of the journey, which means that there aren't too many hard-and-fast rules to live by. Depending on your upbringing, you may have just chucked out the guidebook altogether in search of a different set of instructions. So instead of requiring a fully formed sense of your new self, which might just be impossible at this stage, the Magician offers a more malleable way forward: Play with your sense of self the way that a child would! Dress up! Experiment with colors, fabrics, and textures! Get a new look! Get a tattoo! Cut your hair! Buy new hair! Get top surgery! Get bottom surgery! Don't change a thing! Wear makeup! Stop wearing makeup! Touch yourself! Touch and be touched by others! Reclaim, refresh, and realize the magic of your physical body!

The summer after editing that fateful Tinder profile, I visited my hometown to share the changes I was making in my dating life with my mom and my best friends. Everyone was incredibly supportive, which I do not take for granted, and with that rare and radical love behind me, I did what any baby bisexual would do—I chopped off my hair, bought a pair of overalls, and played around with acting less "feminine." Sure, it was stereotypical, but it was also my most honest attempt to embody my surfacing self. I was modeling what I had witnessed from the queer people who had come before me, employing the long-established method of *observational learning*. Monkey see, monkey do. It wasn't where I ultimately landed, as a person or an aesthetic, but giving myself permission to look and move in new ways was a freeing and empowering first step of discovery.

The Magician also reminds us that *belief* is integral to magic. To work with the tarot, you must believe in what you are doing and believe that it will have an effect, even if you never see the outcome. Belief is also at the core of the emerging self. You must believe in who you are becoming and believe that it is worth your while to continue to find out who that is.

Whenever the time comes, or when looking back on the version of yourself that was brave enough to get your gay ass out there, may you be bold and creative and courageous. May every single preference, kink, quirk, and character trait propel you forward into your new life. The one that you've been dreaming of, even if you never imagined the details to look like this. The one that you've been walking toward, always, even if you didn't recognize the path. The one that's meant for you, on your own timeline.

May the Magician welcome you to who you are *now*.

Four of Wands

The Four of Wands represents the joyful execution of a solid plan. It's a peek behind the curtain at all the tedious planning that went into making the party happen. But as tempting as it might be to watch the festivities from the safe and supportive sidelines, the Four of Wands pushes you out onto the dance floor, encouraging you to experience joy and pleasure before the strike of midnight turns you back into a pumpkin.

When I first started exploring my queerness, I found a lot of identity and certainty in the label of *bisexual*. It felt like a flag that I could stake into the ground. A nametag to wear that would help others know me, find me, and connect with me. I even went so far as to host a podcast about it with a friend and colleague, on which we explored different facets of the bisexual experience, such as the in-community stereotype of "stopping *bi* on the way to gay," how poorly bisexuals are portrayed in the media, and how it feels to be in a monogamous relationship while still supporting your bisexual partner's continued self-exploration. It felt relevant and important, this work of connection through communal dissection.

The Four of Wands invokes the feeling of being enclosed in a canopy of fairy lights, dancing a jig of celebration. A label can feel like this, too. It can feel like you finally have words to express who you are, who you love, and where you belong. Even better, it can feel like you've finally joined the party, and that the guests suddenly feel like friends. In a sea of confusion, my first label was my anchor. Fast-forward a couple of years though, and that label started to feel about a size and a half too small. The Four of Wands also wants us to shirk off the too tight, the itchy, and the outdated. Inside our little hearth, there is only warmth. The minute something feels too cold, kick it out into the night.

One day, I started saying that I am *queer*.

Queer seemed to encompass the whole of the attractions I'd felt in my lifetime, which went far beyond the implied binary of the term *bisexual*. I know that many who identify as bisexual today feel that the term is inclusive of many gender identities, and I do believe that to be true. But I'm a word witch, and I couldn't get over it. I also liked the primary definition of queer of "strange; odd," and how that intersected with my other labels of *artist* and *witch*.

Still, the bisexual community was my first safe space, and they will forever be my people. It boils my blood that there are still so many stigmas, misrepresentations, and mistrust around being bisexual, like that it's a phase or an inability to make up one's mind. Despite making up the largest subsection of the LGBTQIA+ umbrella, it's likely due to these judgments that bisexual people are far less likely to be out to their loved ones.[14] So far, I've tried not to let the outside world in too much, for this is a book by and for queer people, and we shouldn't always have to speak about ignorance, hatred, and violence just because others can't seem to let those ancient abstractions go. But to deny their existence is futile, and the barriers they create between people are as real as the new clothes on our backs.

Being queer doesn't guarantee you safety. It doesn't guarantee you housing, or a good job, or a place among your blood relatives, or positive representation, or governmental rights. Depending on when and how you're coming out to yourself or others, you might even wonder if it's even worth it to chance "ruining" one life in hope of building another. However, silencing yourself to protect others is a huge price to pay for "protecting the peace." (*Whose* peace? Certainly not yours.) It's true that being queer means that you might have to construct structures that will support and sustain you when standard systems fail.

This is tough work, but you can do it. I promise you can.

---

14 A. Brown, *5 Key Findings about LGBTQ+ Americans*, Pew Research Center, June 23, 2023, *pew-research.org*.

The Four of Wands asks us to open ourselves to the possibility that your new home, and your newly chosen family, might feel cozier than any you have walked away from. There is an incredibly special quality of kinship between queer people. It's indescribable how it feels to be seen wholly and fully, and to be loved, and cared for, wholly and fully. (I also admit that some of the nastiest situations I've found myself a part of interpersonally have also been with queer people. Humans are humans.) To be able to *be* and express the truest, messiest, in-process goo-self to others, and for that to be championed, holds the sweetest elixir. A healing balm.

Whether the struggle has been external, internal, or both at the same time, every queer person has spent time in deep doubt and questioning. Every queer person has felt unsafe. Every queer person has overcome something to be here with you now. It's like Taylor Swift says about New York: "Everybody here's been someone else before."[15] So, the shared experiences that follow are potent. To trek through the caves of becoming, and to then have the privilege and pleasure of communing with others as you all play, experiment, blossom, and bloom is the kind of *magic* that everyone ought to be able to conjure up and enjoy.

May the Four of Wands assist you in feeling seen and safe.

Seven of Pentacles

The Seven of Pentacles wants to cut right to the chase. This card represents the patience it takes to reach the harvest. It's a slower-moving energy because it engages with evolution in the physical. In the spiritual and mental realms, change can happen in a nanosecond—but Earthly growth is subject to a different experience of time. Down here in the dirt, it takes continued care, effort, and perseverance for things to ripen and be ready.

---

15   Taylor Swift. "Welcome to New York." On *1989*, Taylor Swift/Republic Records, 2023.

After working to both embody your queerness and make those efforts communal, you might be feeling wrung out like a sponge. This is especially true if your outsides don't yet match your insides, or if the accepting chosen family the gays are always talking about hasn't quite shown up yet. Maybe the more you experience mainstream queer culture (whatever that means), the less you feel like you fit there either. This is as valid as it is depleting. It takes physical, mental, and spiritual energy to stay the course when it appears as if nothing is happening. Courage too.

The Seven of Pentacles doesn't promise a return on your investment, but it hopes for one anyway. It tends to what's hazy because it has faith that one day things will become clear. It also implores us to take up the art of *pruning*. Just as clipping away dead and diseased branches is important to the health and vitality of a plant, it is vital to regularly release aspects of ourselves, and our habits and behaviors, that are no longer serving the future we're creating. That energy can then be reclaimed and repurposed. Channeled to different needs. Used to build better and more authentic patterns and routines. Tedious work, indeed, but the more mundane aspects of magic ensure its survival.

Not to mention, it's an action of deep devotion and love to keep going when you feel like giving up.

After almost two full turns of the nine-year wheel spent observing numerological yearly cycles, and countless hours spent analyzing other people's charts, I am confident in saying that the seven year is one of the hardest, if not *the* hardest, year to experience. Seven is the year of The Seeker. It represents questions and analysis, deep sea explorations, and shedding of spiritual skins.

Notice I didn't say questions and *answers*. That's because seven isn't so much bothered with pesky, fallible things like answers, which can change at the drop of a hat. Instead, the energy of seven lies in the journey. The quest. The step-by-step surrender to the unknown. But three hundred and sixty-five days are a lot of days to spend without clarity or certainty. Even with nourishing habits and support systems in place, you may lose faith or start to doubt that you'll even make it to your next destination. By September, you may be ready to pack a bag and head out. You're driving in fog, without a compass or a prayer, and calling it quits looks tempting as hell.

It's called the seven-year itch for a reason.

Nevertheless, you must persist. *We* must persist.

Sometimes I look at my life and think about how different it is from what I imagined it would be when I was growing up. I was never the type to plan my wedding or think about what to name my future kids, but *compulsory heterosexuality* (a term coined by poet Adrienne Rich) insisted that my partner would be a cisgender man.[16] I never considered that I would have a wife, like I never thought that I'd have thirteen tattoos or write smutty fanfic on the internet or be so attached to a small dog whose farts are weapons of mass destruction. And yet, when I think about my wife's sleepy smile, the way it feels to wake up next to her, and how blissful it is to pull that stinky pup up from the foot of the bed for the morning "family snuggle," I believe in intelligent design.

Depending on when you're coming into yourself as a queer person, you may struggle to grasp how you're still not done growing yet. Even when you think you have a handle on things, you may realize that there's more to explore. This could look like outgrowing a label as I did, or maybe your gender isn't as straightforward as you once thought. Once your mind is open to other ways of being and moving through the world, there's no telling where the rabbit hole will bottom out. Maybe it never will.

---

16   A. Rich, "Compulsory Heterosexuality and Lesbian Existence," *Signs* 5, no. 4 (1980): 631–60. jstor.org.

I hope *patience* is a virtue you can create time for. I hope you can find beauty in this endless uncovering. I hope that you can see how gorgeous your continued becoming truly is. I hope that you can stay curious and active in your own growth so that you may not only live to see the harvest but to exalt in it. After all, fruit on the vine ripens, falls, and then dies, whether in the belly or on the ground.

The Seven of Pentacles wants you to live long and strong enough to eat your fill.

No matter when you are coming to know yourself along the path, and no matter what anyone else's drive, speed, or progress looks like, the Magician, the Four of Wands, the Seven of Pentacles, and the whole ass deck want you to chart a course and set out toward your bright and shining future.

Evolutionary, spiritual, magic, mysterious, incendiary, captivating—*queerness* is a never-ending spiral down, and up, and in, and out. It's a dance with the deepest parts of yourself. A constant excavation of your wildest desires, and the return to the surface to bring them to light. See them glow in the warmth of the Sun. Wear them as a badge, a costume, a smile, a wink. Show them off to the scores of folks waiting to welcome you to your new life with open arms.

I can't wait to see you on the road.

THE SLOW LANE SPREAD

Picture this:

You're cruising in your dream car. It's the perfect color on the outside, and the perfect blend of comfort and style on the inside. The radio is blasting a playlist of your favorite songs. The windows are down, and the wind whips pleasantly through your hair. The road is long and winding, but you're taking it at a pace that feels good. The sun is shining overhead and the air smells sweet. You feel confident and centered, and you drive like the car is an extension of you because, in so many ways, it is. You may not know exactly where you're going, but you're enjoying the drive.

For this tarot spread, you'll need a tarot deck of your choosing and something to take notes with. This could be a pen and a journal or a digital tool such as a phone or computer.

Pull out the Magician, the Four of Wands, and the Seven of Pentacles from the deck. As you lay them out in a horizontal line, look at the imagery of each card.

- What do you notice about them, both individually and collectively?
- Is there a shared color scheme?
- Do the cards have figures on them? If so, what do these figures look like? What are they wearing? What actions are they engaged in?
- If not, what else is shown?

Jot down your observations and any feelings that might pop up as you ponder each card.

Take a moment to prepare your space. It might feel lovely to build an altar to your past, present, and future selves, bringing in any symbolic items or pictures to represent you throughout time and space. Maybe you even want to make an offering to your new self, of roses or candies or the promise of a chosen family who loves you just as you are. Permit yourself to season this spread with as little or as much spice as you'd like. You and your deck might just be the only dynamic duo necessary. Trust your (grieving) (growing) gut.

When you feel ready, call in your guides, ancestors, angels, and any characters from books or movies that you would like to be present with you for clarity, guidance, and support. If you're newer to all this or are experiencing a loss of spiritual connections as a part of your evolution, there's no need to petition anyone in particular. Simply ask for protection and clarity along your journey.

Take a deep breath, in through the nose and out through the mouth. Begin to shuffle your cards, continuing to pay attention to your breath as it moves through your body. Read the following prompts, aloud or silently, and then prepare to pull in whatever way feels right to you.

1. Your emerging self
2. Actions you can take to support this evolution
3. What you may need to grieve or recover from as you shed your previous skin
4. Ways to make the transition more fun
5. How to connect with others as your new self
6. Spiritual advice for building internal safety
7. Practical advice for building external safety
8. An ally of grace when the going gets tough
9. A reminder of the fulfilling future you're creating

Take any notes that you need to, including imagery that shows up, any references that might come to mind, quotes that pop in, or anything else you'd like to return to later. If you simply want to sit in silence with your cards, that's okay too. Trust that whatever you need to know or remember will return to you in another fashion.

Close out your space with gratitude. Give thanks to any spiritual support that you received, as well as your deck and the three allies that will continue to love up on you as you venture forward. Finally, thank your selves for showing up, and for being brave enough to explore these deep waters of self. May you continue to bring your hidden treasures to the surface, and may they continue to lead you in the direction of authenticity, love, and belonging.

So be it, so it is.

THE HIGH PRIESTESS AS BLACK FEMME MEMORY

By Junauda Petrus

i am accused of tending to the past as if i made it,
as if i sculpted it
with my own hands. i did not.
this past was waiting for me
when i came ...

—Lucille Clifton

The witch, the sweetener, the lover, the runaway witch, Oya. The High Priestess/High Priestexx is a queer, Black feminist wild woman and spiritual devotee. She is butt naked and shea-buttered up under her immaculate powder blue and velvet robes. She got a g-string made of pearls. She got lovers that she texts with a burning candle emoji asking for them to give her a slow burn kind of love. The High Priestess likes sweet, soft, thick nut-brown lips grazing her body, just so, like that ... with attention and intention. She likes long and oily massages and to play Marvin Gaye falsetto all day, some days. She is the temple, the pum pum palace, the erotic enclave of eternal embodiment. *She is us* wandering naked in someone's forest under the moon, howling an open-sky sonar toward some kind of inner home. Next to her feet (in all-black Chuck Taylors) is the crescent moon, and it is a wink and a glimpse at the spiritual undergrounds that dwell within her that we see in the Moon card.

High Priestess as the Young Wild Self (Black Emo Outside Girl)

The Moon card is the hood that the High Priestexx, aka HP, grew up in—a place of frequent darkness and beautiful shadow, where everyone sits on their stoops at night, or lay on the tar beaches of their apartment building, or walk to the corner store for peach soda and cheese sandwiches with bbq chips. Let's consider them from a young age, a trickster, and curious. The High Priestexx is a young and flat-chested tomboy, quiet and pensive, repeating poetry to theyself. They walk down the street under the moon's cool illumination and smell the whiff of cinnamon-scented blunts amid the vibrating speakers playing SWV at her uncle's house party. The High Priestess wasn't always dwelling at the gates of the temple, as much as she was the temple itself, absorbing all of the life in her world, into the archives of her skin and limbs.

The High Priestess when she was a small child wandered the hood of her community until it became forest, waters, and trees. Where and how she grew up was a place that understood and respected all of the energies of creation as sacred and belonging.

Quiet as it's kept, the HP is the magician's big sister/sibling, who taught her baby brother that all things contain potential and mystery and to wield that with all of the tenderness and reverence you got. Always moving fast, smooth, and a little sweaty, they taught him how to commune with anything from frog to flower to the elders who are condensed deep, living monasteries themselves. Our High Priestess, as a child, was given permission to be in tune to the intelligence of her body's intuition. To hold a leaf and feel inside of her body, whether it was poison or medicine or magic. To know what the sky said when it spoke in veins of fire and light, or was gray purple with all the feelings, or was peppered with meditations of visions with cloud patterns of divination, and haikus and Sanskrit and song. The High Priestess learned from they grandmama what the earth said when you put it between your fingers and felt the tightness and thickness of her. Her dry, her muddy, her wet. What were the places that the herbs, grains, roots, yam, and cassava could grow and when? Everything in creation said something to the High Priestess when they was a kid because they listened. Her feral nature was never asked to close its legs, to get small. She was not told to save it till marriage or deny her body. They was allowed to touch theyself in they own wet wilderness and feel the dream of their own body, tremor and electrify under they own touch.

The High Priestexx is the many levels that soul and magic can be born from attempts to destroy and erase the power of the oppressed. The common story of the High Priestess comes from that of "The Popess," the female pope who was put into power and then executed once instated. This story has variations and elaborations, but the essence of it is simple. The Popess, like many witches of that time and this, was burned at the stake for the simple fact of being not-man and pillow-talking with the divine. The High Priestexx is the essential witch of the tarot, teaching us that a witch is nothing but a femme/nonbinary soul who lives in direct communication with the divine wildness that exists in all of creation without the permission or participation of patriarchy. Their access to an internal divine audience as a femme/nonbinary is what makes them a threat to the patriarchy and a baddie in general. They sip the tea of the supernatural and make enough for us all to partake.

The HP is different in that they let us know we have desire: intellectual desire, emotional desire, the soulful desire to know ourselves within our own erotic, and its sacred specificity. The HP lets us know that we want to be spanked, worshipped, licked, stroked, and teased, and be a submissive little kitten or be a thick-assed domme daddy in consensual authority or left the fuck alone—that we have shadows, that we fall apart, and that we want to be gathered. The High Priestess I imagine is all of the juiciness of our spiritual energies that live on the inside of our erotic depths. I dream and remember how ancient her existence is, and ever returning and cycling back through time and space, to reveal to us that we are a revelation. The High Priestexx was there for me as a teen queer kid, whispering to my emo and despair-filled existence and told me to read poetry and cry and feel feelings, to touch myself, to lay among the trees and hear their whispers, to dance naked in moonlight. The HP is the official patron deity of the emo outsider kid.

High Priestess as That 'Round the Way Sista Who I Wanted to Know and Be

I realized the High Priestess was the one I was looking for when I would be in African dance classes in Harlem in the mid 2000s. I'd smell her frankincense and Florida water amid the rhythmic hurricane of her enchantment. She grooved past me, locs and limbs swinging to a rhythm all her own that I wanted to get inside of. She was someone I wanted to lick. She was the one with a bag full of books about hidden mystical things, a diary of poetry she had written in purple ink, a tupperware of sliced pineapple and some crystals she kept on her for when she is in her feelings. She is the type that got tinctures, ginger chews, and tea tree oil for anything you need to heal right quick, *and* she got a tarot deck, just in case we all out at the park and someone heartbroken (or just broke period) and they need some guidance. She got a scarf made of African fabric wrapped like a whirlwind around her neck and a coat that is part cape and part blanket vortex.

Or maybe she is dressed up, eyeliner on fleek and lipstick popping, ready for the club, looking like a snack, sitting with herself on the subway, eyes blinked close in the particular glow of subway fluorescence, her prayer beads in hand mouthing a silent prayer, mantra, gospel for some kind of intention, invocation, irritation.

She was the one at community college who was in the cosmetic school, who knew I was in love with her within the clumsy over-affection of my friendship. She invited me to come over, and when we talked late into the sensual hours, she told me I could spend the night and let me sleep in her bed and we made love all night. I was looking for her because I wanted to make sense of my inside self, the part of me that felt like a secret, the part of me that felt things deeply and intuitively and was afraid of feeling alone in the spiritual journey of myself.

As a child, I was attracted to those women who were witchy, different, stood out, didn't fit in. There was a mystery and enigmaticness to them that felt connected to cosmic truths. I longed to have someone take me up under their cape and tell me they had a dream about me. The very existence of these women allowed me to make sense within myself. I wanted to be snuck somewhere amid her soft and cluttered earthy-sweet-musk-smelling interior, into her indigo velvet self, her inky limitlessness and be reminded that something in me is a never-ending mystery. That there are layers of ancient knowledge nestled into my DNA and swept up and inside of juicy desire. I wanted to sip tea with her in her boudoir and hear her truths, her secrets, and the vibration of her vibrant flesh.

High Priestess as Domme

Equal part domme and spiritual devotee, the HP is the devotion to our erotics that are within our spiritual path that was colonized and oppressed out of our lineage. I'm delving into understanding and acknowledging the HP in a way that brings them closer into me, my world, and my experience.

In this meditation of the High Priestess, I feel them as a limitless multitude of queer, mysterious, and beyond comprehension revelation.

She reminds me that we are worthy of our own worship, our own pleasuring and satisfying. I inverse this into the church girl, who loves the (Audre) Lorde and loves to fuck—a spirituality not divorced from sensuality, and the way that we have been forced to live that dichotomy in modern times. In thinking about the High Priestess and her/their queerness, I think of what writer and King Muva, Alexis De Veaux, contemplates in her own multidimensional creativity, about being "less concerned of who is queer, but more so on what is queer." The High Priestess simultaneously queers, sensualizes, and interrogates the church in their existence. Her church is C.H.U.R.C.H. Come Here U Rebel Come Here. They remember and remind us of the ways of the ancestors, of wildness and the erotic and the temple of the self.

The High Priestess/Priestexx will tell us the spell to surface the secret of our own country (coochie)[17]. The Priestexx is as much a steward of the divine secrets as they are the divine secret itself. She symbolizes the sacred elixirs prismed within us, through our ancestral lines that we feel at the phantom edges of our lives and our unconsciousness. They are the restraint and the release. She knows that spirit and sensuality and erotic are not meant to be separate, that our bodies hold the cosmology of all things. The High Priestess knows spirit and desire. The High Priestexx has a sexuality that is turned on by philosophy, spirituality, and nature's reflections.

The High Priestess as Black Femme Divine Vessel

Before I began studying tarot, I was introduced to Nina Simone as the "High Priestess of Soul," and on a subconscious level I've always syncretized the High Priestess with something Black, feminist, and other worldly. The words *High* and *Priestess* speak to her gravity as

---

[17] I use *coochie* here in the queer semantics lineage of reimagining of *pussy*, *cunt*, and other euphemisms as beyond anatomical definition and instead within an expansive energetic vortex that resides in the soft folds of our middle and wet selves.

a musician being something more than musical, but a spiritual and transcendent offering and prayer. Nina Simone's voice was the activation of gospel and Africa and Black and woman and unwavering truth, a primordial self that is undeniable. Simone, as the High Priestess of Soul, like many Black artists in the diaspora, brought the Black Church and its gospel of continuance and wizardry, in their throat, heart, and tongue. In the Black Church, Simone received her musical, spiritual, and social justice foundation, and got to study with the musical virtuosos of her community. And like the High Priestess, Simone wasn't understood or fully held in her truth sharing, her witness and wisdom being seen as a problem and thus shunned.

The Black Church (the terriero, the Ile, the houses of ballroom) is where African spiritualities were ensconced, hidden, and alchemically glorified within the religion our ancestors' captors forced and enforced on them. The Black Church is an intersectional lineage of African mysticism and the spiritual innovation of the oppressed. Africans, stolen, then spiritually persecuted and villainized, alchemized a religion meant to brainwash and enslave them and made it into technology for liberation. In the cosmology of the Black diaspora, the High Priestess is witnessed and expressed within the femmes and nonbinary who were able to hold on to all of the sacred spirituality of our ancestors amid middle passage, deracination and bondage, and resuscitate it back to life and transmute it for our purposes here.

When I think of the High Priestess in this particular dimension of the Black femme divine vessel, I think of the lyrical penetration and gospel grit of so many singers (sangers), musicians who know how to feel things and help us feel things alongside them: Aretha Franklin, Luther Vandross, Whitney Houston, Anita Baker, Sun Ra, Sade, Marvin Gaye, Sylvester, Celia Cruz, Tina Turner, Bessie Smith, Yolanda Adams, Jimi Hendrix, Prince, Lauryn Hill, Miriam Makeba, Alice Coltrane, and all a dem and then some who felt the Black and the feelings and had to High Priestess it out of themselves. Gathered the feelings from feet to coochie to falsetto to the hmmmm and moan and yessss and soaked us in the divine love that we are and that wants to speak to us. These voices resonated with the shake, depth, and light of God herself and channeling the frequency of the High Priestess in themselves and being the moonlight we can walk into.

High Priestess as Octavia Butler, June Jordan, Lucille Clifton, Prophet Moon Women

There are other worlds (they have not told you of)
They wish to speak to you
—Sun Ra, "There Are Other Worlds"

She sings, whispers, channels, invites us over the dragging yet syncopated drum kit. An eerie moaning, part siren's call of hypnosis. Part scary, part meditative bass. What are the other worlds? Are they ancestral, alien? I have to delve within my internal, unfathomable, vastness, darkness, that I've always felt teetering and confused on the shore of my consciousness. Is the other worlds a place of crazy or alchemy? If Octavia Butler was a song, it would be this particular Sun Ra song. Is this other world God/dess, or whatever concept of the divine, high expansive, all encompassing, cosmic, ultragalactic, ineffability? Or an energy, a feeling that you just know in your marrow self?

The High Priestess within her elements has written the stories and oral histories down from all of the grandmothers she knew and others she channeled. Octavia Butler's words and stories are one-part speculative imagination and prophetic dreaming of the world that was being unfolded in the legacy of the violence of white patriarchal settler domination. She told us and then sipped her tea.

Lucille Clifton started channeling after her mom sashayed to the other side of the veil, and still was able to gossip and gospel with her daughter. She was just an ancestral telephone call away and still had things to say, and Lucille had things to know for herself and the world.

Listening in this world and feeling in other worlds, other dimensions. It began with using Ouija boards to feel for her mama, hands grasping behind the glittery opaque veil protecting the sanctity of this world and the next place, other worlds. Her life and home became a temple for the spiritual technology of listening into other realms and with the ancestors and other celestial beings.

> *"Two-headed woman" is a traditional African American term used to describe women gifted with access to the spirit world as well as to the material world.*
> —Marina Magloire, *Paris Review*, October 2020

After the Ouija, Lucille then used her pen to access her other head, her other mind, and write what was being said in the dialect of her poetry and feelings.

June Jordan was a lover and a warrior and a lover and a lover and a lover. Because what is the revolution with the love, the honey, the sweetness, and the vision and the dream? This ain't on the spiritual bypassing. It's in the depth of the feels, in the vulnerability, in the looking directly into the pain and telling the truth and feeling the truth you speak. She was that High Priestess love in the way she fought for us and all people to be free, to live in the soft of their homelands and not genocided. A Black woman, from Brooklyn and from the islands of her parents, she became a Palestinian and a love language for revolution. She saw the constellation of the oppression and read us a horoscope of freedom, with a tongue of machete and a heart of honeycomb.

I once got to read her letters in an archive to one of her lovers. A man fourteen years younger than her, a married poet who knew the wildness of her heart and clarity of her vision for the world and loved sipping on the elixir of her mind and body. In one letter, she was writing on her birthday, July 9 (the same birthday as me), and she was by the ocean and listening to an Earth, Wind & Fire album and was loving it. I imagine her feet up and she is wearing something light and silky and she just had a cup of coffee and it was sweet. Her thighs are epiphany. She feeling in love with her ownself and juicy with that love.

My King Muva, Alexis De Veaux, was a friend of hers when June was on this side of the veil, and said that June was a gangsta in that Black proverbial way of "don't start no stuff won't be no stuff" or we getting on the subway and pulling up and finishing it, mainly with her lovers. June Jordan was a lover and a warrior and a lover and a lover and a lover.

Octavia Butler, Lucille Clifton, and June Jordan, all born under the sign of Cancer, the crab, the pearl, the shelled warrior with the soft insides, protecting the tender in them and us. The children who was born feeling the moon and water and the messages of soul that seep in from the invisible realms, that are other worlds, that wish to speak to us.

Octavia, Lucille, and June are all of the pages of the tarot, page of burning light and passion (Wands), page of intellectual movement and breeze (Swords), page of sensation and commitment (Pentacles), page of intuition and feeling (Cups). Doing their studies in their bodies and souls, holding all of the places of our expansive humanity, then conveying to us all the depths and complexities of this world. World builders from the realms of the silenced and erased, their perspectives were elixirs for survival. A moon woman, priestesses of pen, and we needed their channels and transmissions to feel into the beyonds. The beyond of this reality, beyond the veils, beyond all that has been written for us to know.

High Priestess as Shug Avery

All the men got they eyes glued to Shug's Bosom. I got my eyes glued there too. I feel my nipples harden under my dress. My little button sort of perk up too. Shug, I say to her in mind, Girl, you looks like a good time, the Good Lord knows you do.

—Alice Walker, *The Color Purple*

In Alice Walker's *The Color Purple*, Celie confides in her new best friend, Shug Avery, that she has never liked sex ever in her life. Shug Avery is shocked about this since she personally loves sex so much, especially with Celie's husband, Mr. _____, who was Shug's baby daddy and most passionate lover. Celie insists that the whole act of sex has always felt like a man "doing his business in you" and that it never felt pleasurable. Shug asks Celie about her clitoris, which she calls a button, and then begins to walk Celie through witnessing her own pussy by looking at it in a mirror. Celie was raped and impregnated by her stepdaddy and then forced to marry an abusive, brokenhearted widower, Mr._____. Celie, in the eyes of the men who ran her life, was never supposed to have pleasure or even desire it. And here go Shug Avery showing Celie her "button" and telling her she deserves pleasure and juiciness. The two tender friends become tender lovers in an unlikely love story between a wife and her husband's mistress. Celie and Shug, honeybee and honey.

I think of HP Shug Avery often. A hot mess who loved herself and lived in the sacred practice of centering pleasure in her life. She lived her life draped in beads, feathers, and sequins, lingerie and silk kimonos, a cigarette dangling off her fingers, a bedazzled priestess of sensual and erotic realms. You ever seen somebody who is living a life that is complicated, beautiful, luxurious, wild, and unapologetic . . . and just fell in love with them? They invite you inside them and its vast, velvet, smelling of fresh rain, orange peel, frankincense, and sweet soft kisses. They ask you to come close to them, and they are skin and silk and invitation to remember and forget and taste and beg for the relief and the education of pleasure. Shug was nothing if not Celie's priestess to the erotic.

> Shug come over and she and Sofia hug. Shug say, Girl, you look like a good time, you do. That when I notice how Shug talk and act sometimes like a man. Men say stuff like that to women, Girl,

you look like a good time. Women always talk about hair and health. How many babies living or dead or got teef. Not about how the woman they hugging look like a good time.[18]

Shug lived in the liminal gender nonconformity and pansexuality that was the way of Indigenous and African ancestors. In this new world, this postbellum reality in which she was defining her boundaries and invitations with lovers. She was a wayward woman, a whore. A Black woman who slept with and shared her body with who pleased and pleasured herself was a whore. The white man had colonized the land's body, soul, and suppleness. The white man had enslaved and created a culture of professional rape to round out their work force and slaveocracy. There was no democracy in a slaveocracy or post unhealed pseudo-slaveocracy, which is America, which is the world. Bessie Smith, Ma Rainey, and all of the Black blues women were the high priestesses of feeling and sacral longing, of naming their abuse in a world run by men and white people, of their yearning and curated lovers, of their queerness. Yes, most of them were gay as hell, loved fluidly, and dressed in clothes of women and men and whatever felt right.

The blues woman as High Priestess was a spirit in the room, was an energetic and erotic hurricane forcing everyone to contend with what choices they were making to live a life that satisfied something insatiable and unanswerable. Shug resisted the pathways to survival and protection within the world she was born into. She didn't aspire to be a wife, a mama, or even respectable. She wanted to feel her life, and make it honey and wetness and wild and dirty and truth all around her. She was going to decide what her life was going to be. And she was a lover and she loved men and women too much to try and love either exclusively.

We look at the blues for the way it tells the truth, the gospels of the honest self and of Black life, of the oppression, pain, hurt, and heartbreak that we as Black folks feel, but ain't even supposed to acknowledge. The

---

18 Alice Walker, *The Color Purple* (Penguin, 1982).

blues woman keeps it a stack and tells us her truth, that she wants to be loved and licked and not be nobody's help, or sharecropper or slave. In the High Priestess as blues woman, you can see the spiritual devotee that she is. The blues was where our true feelings bubbled up from somewhere deep inside where they had to be all hid and disappeared. We had to be robots, invisible, obedient, domesticated animals, objects that absorb all of the scars and transmute it into labor and silence. Our existence was one big gaslight over generations and eras. For Black folks the Church and the blues is where we got to be humanized and sacred. We got to moan, cry, and emote all of the truth of our insides without interference and management from our white captors and enslavers. But the life lived in devotion to the blues that Shug Avery chose was seen as an affront to the religious and respectable life, the life that granted Black people worth in the eyes of white people and our greater society. The blues confessed all of our truths in a way that we couldn't deny. The blues revealed that we as Black people were sentient and soulful beings and felt every last horrible thing that was done to us and those we loved. That we missed our lovers and family when they sold or killed them. The blues denied the premise of slavery that we as a people were so physically strong and impenetrable, and our minds so base, that our pain and our sense of spirituality was nonexistent. Our physical bondage was rebranded as our spiritual liberation, by white enslavers and missionaries. The blues responds back, teaching us waywardness and access to pleasure, love, and heartbreak that is our human curriculum to figure out existential and cosmic wisdoms.

***

> *The priestess is also known as the oracle. She stares deep into your soul with the look of inner knowing and from her place of ancient memories and deep mysteries, she summons you. From her you will receive assistance on your quest.*[19]

---

[19] Mary K. Greer, *Tarot For Yourself*, Anniversary ed. (Weiser Books, 2019), 76.

Whenever I pull tarot and the High Priestess shows up, I feel ease and a tingle in my coochie, I'm not gonna lie. The witch in all of her phases: from a wildling child self, to a teen, angsty and transforming self, to a soft clay learning how to shape herself. The hot and bothered PILF (priestess I'd like to fuck) clad in mesh, leather straps, velvet capes, and dripping in pleasure possibilities. The HP is raining in pleasure, intoxicated in their own vibrating and honey-dipped gravity, and the ripening and intensity and the spreading out and the crystallizing and the self knowledge. She is me, she is us, and the part of us that feels behind and in the depths of our own interior lush and velvet temples of self and is healing and revelation.

THE EMPRESS

By Maria the Arcane

Humming to herself, the Empress strolls through the castle of her design as she makes her way to her destination. As she does, she takes in the beautiful place she has cultivated, not only for herself but for the people she treasures the most—the artists, artisans, philosophers, dreamers, and beautiful creatures she calls her court, friends, and charges.

The castle itself is surrounded by nature, and with it being springtime, the numerous large windows and balconies show off Mother Earth in all of her glory. The large oak trees, the wildflowers in the distance, and the immaculately kept gardens are their own unique pieces of art displayed through panes of glass and iron framework. It not only fits perfectly in this castle she calls home, but especially in her personally accumulated art gallery, her destination, and one of her temples (the other being on the other side of the panes of glass).

As the Empress opens up the large and ornate doors, the scent of fresh paint greets her. Immediately, her eyes drift toward the ceiling with glee and awe. On the ceiling are bodies swimming amongst the heavens. The blue sky and clouds cradle all the beautiful and diverse figures. Deliciously curvy, elflike, warrior, or middling bodies are all delicately draped in painted satin or free of any veils, naked and unafraid. Many were embracing, caressing, or just enjoying themselves, each of them free of any restraints placed on them by society's strict standards, including those of gender and sexuality. She has spared no expense, and you could tell by all the detail giving these forms life. Dimples, rolls, scars, and flesh-lightning strikes are on full display. She gently brushes a tear off her cheek before she walks over to the artist whose magic hands painted this grand manifestation of life and beauty. *"Truly a celebration that everyone should be having,"* she thinks.

A little voice in the back of her mind whispers, *"as should you."*

As the artist walks away with a look of well-earned triumph on their face, the Empress once again gazes upward. These people of paint and lacquer, for a second time, make her breath hitch, and truth be told, also make her heart ache.

How the Empress longs to be free. To be dressed in loose satin instead of these heavy constricting garments. To be able to show off the sensual creature she is and not the chaste and obedient image and role that have been cast upon her all of her life.

She is the queen of queens, she tells herself out loud. She should be able to do as she damn well pleases. She gives so much of herself to others, why shouldn't she give some back unto herself? To be just as she is. It is her divine right.

An idea sparks.

She asks one of her nearby courtesans to ask the artist to return and to meet her in the study as soon as possible to discuss a new creation. A personal piece.

Out on a field draped in satin that is embellished with pomegranates (a symbol of her transformation and for once choosing herself, much like Persephone), the Empress lounges on cushions, scepter in hand, and her golden hair supporting a crown of stars ready to show herself stepping into her power of divine sensuality as the painter puts brush to canvas.

In this painting, her body is her altar. An altar of her sexuality and gender expression, of freedom and growth. A symbol of her devotion and support of this newfound energy she wants to cultivate for years to come. It is an energy she wants to inspire others to also express their own gender and sexuality in a way that is meaningful and validated.

She closes her eyes and breathes in the scent of the earth, feels the humidity from the waterfall behind her, and listens to the rustle of the stalks of wheat, which is almost ready to be harvested, in front of her. She feels at home. At peace. She is free.

When the painting is complete and sent to her palace, she has it hung up in her bedroom above a long table. Having it here in this spot will remind her what she is cultivating in her life, which is love and acceptance of who she is and her identity.

When her eyes drift over it late one evening and then to the table below it, she feels pulled to decorate the area around it to give the portrait more life and presence. She places her wash basin onto the center of the table, pink candles and roses on the sides, and a fruit bowl full of ripe pomegranates ready to be opened.

She realizes when she is done that she has created an altar. Energy radiates off it; she feels it over every inch of her body. She realizes she has, without meaning to, created a portal to her dreams of cultivating a better relationship with herself.

Breaking Down The Empress Card

Now that we have connected with the energy of the Empress through a story of her awakening (which is important so that we can see the magick prevalent in this card), let us look at her in the *Rider-Waite-Smith* tarot deck. We're using this version because it's the most widely known and utilized, but for any of the future exercises, please use any deck that the Empress card resonates with you the most.

When you pull this card out of the RWS deck, you will see someone lounging upon cushions out in nature in a pomegranate-printed dress. A wheat field is in front of her, and behind her there is a waterfall and a line of trees. Our empress sits knees apart, head held high, a crown of stars on her head, a scepter in her right hand, and a stone heart under her chair that has the sign for Venus (which is also a symbol commonly used to say female, and how I use it here to develop my own story[20]) carved into it.

Now it is easy to look at this card and dismiss it as just feminine energy, but it isn't just that. While it does show what she uniquely identifies with and that she is proud of it, she is also a maternal figure who wants others to feel comfortable with themselves and their unique identities as much as she. She is open to experiences and different perspectives, which we can see because her knees are far apart and she is looking directly at us.

The pomegranate dress plays an important role in this card for me. It links her with the Greek goddess Persephone. While we will not go into the full story of Persephone, I feel it is important to touch on it. When her tale is looked at through a nonmisogynistic lens, it is a story of choosing one's self, transformation, finding personal power, self-acceptance, and of cycles. Persephone was told her whole life who she ought to be; as Kore (her identity before her transformation), she was meant to be a virgin goddess. When eating the seeds in her previous identity as Kore, Persephone is fully stepping into her true self. She is claiming her rightful title and identity as the goddess of the underworld. Goddess of transformation. She claims her true identity and sexuality/sensuality. While she may be the Goddess of Spring still, she takes that title and makes it her own.

I feel many queer people may find her lore relates to their own journeys. The myth, for myself, truly resonates with the discovery of my own sexuality. As a pansexual woman, I had to go on my own inner journey when the time was right to uncover this about myself. Claiming my identity, just as Persephone did, was life-changing. I claimed my

---

20 Editor's note: Remember, these essays are not meant to be prescriptive and are instead each writer telling you how they found themselves in the tarot. Please swap out any pronouns or gendered words that don't work for you as you read if you feel like you need to.

power and found an amazing source of self-love. This is another trait of our Empress, who loves to take care and treat herself to the finer things in life when she needs to.

All of this makes the Empress card the perfect card to utilize when you are going on your own journey of claiming your sexuality, sensuality, and gender identity. She is a champion of being yourself, claiming it, and letting it fuel your inner growth. After all, we grow and become the best versions of ourselves when we work toward self-acceptance and self-love (which is additionally shown on this card by the wheat field, the tree line, and the waterfall).

So go on, grab your favorite Empress card. Let us build a metaphorical throne of our identities and sit upon it in comfort, openness, and radical acceptance.

Creating Altars and Magick for Sexuality and Gender Expression with The Empress

Altars are a great way to help us manifest and harness energy for an extended period of time. An altar is a place where we create a portal and a home for our personal magick.

Before you start thinking that it has to be this grand and beautiful thing, it doesn't! An altar can be small and even as nondescript as you would like it to be. For myself, there are no rules when it comes to setting one up. It is a collection of items that resonate with me spiritually or items handpicked for the specific purpose it was built.

While it is great to have one larger working altar, having small ones around the home for different intentions is a great way to add additional magick into your life. These altars can be temporary or something you honor every so often, but the more time you spend with these specific altars will help bring their purpose alive easier.

For the rest of this chapter, we will create two different altars working with the Empress card as inspiration. These altars will act as portals for developing self-compassion, learning to love our gender/sexuality/sensuality, sparking new personal growth, and even finding beauty in one's life/body. One of the altars will be a physical one in your home, and the other is your moveable and permanent home—your body.

I thought it was poignant to have both. Not many people consider their body a possible altar, but it truly can be! We dress it, put ornaments on it, and coat it in magickal elixirs. It is the perfect space that we are aware of at all times and put energy toward it each and every single day, even in times of low energy.

The Physical Altar

While this altar can be placed anywhere it resonates, I would personally put this one in either a bedroom or bathroom. Places of sensuality and where we typically spend time reflecting on the themes of gender and sexuality when we are alone are going to work best for this altar.

As I have previously mentioned, altars are deeply personal and unique to the person. If any of the things I recommend don't resonate within your practice for your Empress altar, don't incorporate them. Take what resonates and leave what doesn't.

As we build our altars, we must remember that the Empress is a lady of comfort, luxury, sensuality, and growth, all of which she is eager to share with you. We want our physical altars to represent those energies.

I propose using the Empress card as a focal point somewhere on the altar, either by printing off a photo of the card or using one from a deck onto a cardholder. She will serve as a visual reminder of what the altar is for, what you want to cultivate. If that doesn't at all resonate with you, that is okay! When it comes to cultivating an altar space, you are the artist, the creator. Her spirit can be very much there without having an obvious visual representation of her there.

Here are some ideas to add to your altar!

While many of these are based in general symbolism involving the Empress card, a few are my own personal correspondences for the materials. Please take what resonates and leave what doesn't.

A SATIN(ESQUE) OR VELVET SCARF OR ALTAR MAT

Our Empress is an Empress of luxury after all. This scarf or mat will correspond to your altar as a source of comfort and a soft landing when exploring and embracing your identity.

PINK CANDLES

The color pink symbolizes self-love.

GREEN CANDLES

The color green symbolizes internal growth.

GOLD/BRONZE/SILVER ACCENT PIECES

These metals symbolize self-worth.

SYMBOLS OR IMAGERY OF YOUR IDENTITIES

These symbols or images provide a visual representation of the self-love and acceptance that you want to cultivate around them.

CHOCOLATE

Chocolate symbolizes comfort, especially comfort in one's internal self. I get this correspondence from why we tend to gravitate to chocolate: delicious and sweet comfort.

POMEGRANATES

As I mentioned while speaking about the symbolism of the pomegranate in regards to Persephone, pomegranates are a symbol of transformation, radical self-acceptance, and claiming of your personal power.

WATER

There are a lot of emotions tied into the journey of acceptance and self-love. Not all of them are easy to get through. Water serves as a reminder that your emotions are valid; any tears you shed are valid. We can also use water to symbolize washing away the identities placed upon us by society to reveal our own. Regardless, the element of water is very important when it comes to growth. We see that in nature, which is gloriously displayed on the Empress card.

WHEAT

We see wheat featured on the Empress card. Not only a symbol of growth and comfort, wheat is also self-pollinating. It is, at its heart, nonbinary. It stimulates its own growth and reproduction, not needing any of its compatriots' help to do so, which makes it a perfect plant to work with when it comes to sexuality and gender expression.

SAFFRON

This spice is known to be sensual and sexy, an aphrodisiac, which is the correspondence we will look at when adding this to our altars. Alternatively and strangely opposite, it is also a great plant to work with if you are exploring the paths of being asexual! Saffron actually reproduces asexually.

MOTHERWORT

The maternal archetype is very prevalent on the Empress card. I find that many in the queer community struggle with the maternal archetype due to real-world reasons, all of which are valid. If that is the case, think of this energy as that friend who cares and nurtures you. Someone who is the epitome of loving and protective energy. This is what motherwort symbolizes. Its correspondences make it a fierce protector and nurturer. We see these correspondences in its medicinal aspects and lore—how it is good for the heart and serves as a protector magickally speaking for anxiety and even baneful energies.

PINK ROSES, THORNS INTACT

These roses symbolize protecting and blossoming within your journey of self-love and acceptance.

RED ROSES, THORNS INTACT

These roses symbolize protecting and blossoming on your sensual/sexuality journey.

BIRCH BARK

This beautiful tree is a symbol of perpetual and continuous transformation through its bark. Bark strips off, revealing the deepest layer of skin on the tree. When using this on your altar, you will work with it for its transformative nature as well as an ally to reveal your true identities.

ROSE QUARTZ

This classic pink crystal is most often used to promote self-love.

RHODONITE

This crystal depicting unique shapes of different shades of pinks and blacks helps us embrace our uniqueness from a place of self-love.

How to Interact with This Altar

As I have mentioned, the more we interact and form a relationship to our altars, the more we can bring what we are manifesting to life. Having an altar in a spot like a bedroom or bathroom makes it easy, as we are in these rooms often. Interacting with these spaces doesn't have to be time-consuming or energy-draining, so if you are worried about that, I'm here to ease your mind!

Here are some ways you can interact with your altar, ordered from low energy to requiring more energy!

- **Take a moment at the altar** to close your eyes and to envision the intention you are cultivating with it *or* remember why you set it up in the first place if you struggle with envisioning.
- **Say an affirmation at it once a day such as, but not limited to . . .**
    - "It is valid to express my identity in a way that is affirming to me."
    - "Fuck homophobia/transphobia. My sexuality/gender identity is worth defending and natural."
    - "I am worthy of expressing my sensuality in a way that makes me feel powerful and sexy."
- **Place beauty products and "potions" at it** to be blessed by the Empress energy. I recommend rosewater with the purpose of cultivating inner beauty, love, protection, and acceptance.
- **Light a candle** with the intention of adding energy to the altar or as a request for light to be shed on your path forward.
- **Leave the energy of the Empress offerings at the altar**, such as but not limited to beautiful objects, sweets, sweet wines, champagne, and letters about your journey.
- **Interact with your water bowl at the altar**, if you decided to have one. Dip your fingers into the water and place them at pulse points with the intention of embodying empress energy. Also, this can act as an offering by refilling it with fresh water often.
- **Pull a divination card for yourself** to help you connect with the Empress mind-set. Leave this card at the altar for the day to truly mull over and take in its answer! Remember "negative cards" are there to help us improve our situations. If we never got them, we would never know when to better ourselves.

- **Journal at the altar or nearby**, especially when journaling in regard to this altar's purpose.

- **Practice automatic writing** with the intention of connecting with the Empress's energy or guides/ancestors who want to help you step into your power and identities. This would also be great when you want to connect with someone who brings loving motherly energy into your life for support and guidance.

- **Perform ritual dance** with the purpose of connecting to your wild and true nature away from judgment and with the purpose of radical self-acceptance and freedom to be who you truly are.

- **Do spell work** geared to self-love, sex, transformation, and how to find your path forward.

You are not limited to these examples! Do whatever feels right! We all have ways of connecting to certain energies. If you have a unique way you want to explore, do it! This altar serves as a judgment-free zone.

Magickal Things to Do at Your Physical Altar
Love and Acceptance for Sensuality/Sexuality/Gender Spell Jar

What you will need:

- A four-ounce jar
- A small square piece of paper
- Something pink to write with
- Birch bark
- Pinch of saffron
- Dried pink rose petals

- ❖ A small sliver of olive branch
- ❖ New or waxing moon water (water that has been left out under the specific moon phases' light to imbue it with its energy)

Pre-spell:

- ❖ Like the Empress, dress in an outfit that makes you feel the most validated toward what you are doing the spell for or just something comfortable/sexy.
- ❖ Cleanse your space thoroughly in a method that resonates with you. I recommend burning some of the rose petals in a cauldron around the area you'll be performing the spell in with the intention to not only cleanse the space but to also invite self-love in!
- ❖ Cleanse the jar you will be using with smoke or salt water, especially if it is a reused spell jar.

The spell:

- ❖ Call the corners in a way that resonates with you. If you are in your sacred space and feel safe within it, feel free to skip.

Simple way to call the corners turning toward the directions listed:

I call upon the Guardians of the East and of Air to join me in this ritual today.
I call upon the Guardians of the South and of Fire to join me in this ritual today.
I call upon the Guardians of the West and of Water to join me in this ritual today.
I call upon the Guardians of the North and of Earth to join me in this ritual today.
I call upon the Guardians of the Above to join me in this ritual today.

> *I call upon the Guardians of the Below to join me in this ritual today.*
> *I call upon the Guardians of Center to join me in this ritual today.*

- ❖ Now in the center of your paper, write what you need love and acceptance toward. Once you are done, hold this paper in your magickally dominant hand. Your magickally dominant hand is typically your nonwriting hand, and the one you have the most sensation in. Close your eyes, take a deep breath in, a deep breath out, and for a moment envision yourself at your most confident. This can be a memory or just what you aspire to!

Take a deep breath in and a deep breath out. Open your eyes.

With energy and purpose of embracing what you just envisioned, draw a heart around your words. Then fold the paper three times toward you to bring that energy into existence and place it in your jar.

- ❖ As you add these next few ingredients, do so with intention. Intention in this case is remembering the "why" as you add them to your jar—why you are adding these in the first place. Feel free to spend time with each plant envisioning their corresponding keywords manifesting in your life.

> *A sliver of birch bark for personal transformation*
> *A small pinch of saffron to feel sexy and/or confident in your own skin*
> *A very small handful of pink rose petals to grow and cultivate self-love*

- ❖ With your olive branch, hold both ends with your pointer fingers and thumbs. Once again, close your eyes, take a deep breath in, a deep breath out, and offer your words and thoughts of forgiveness. This ingredient is meant to be you extending an olive branch to yourself. Sometimes we can be our own worst critics after all, and queerphobic toward ourselves, when we truly should be our biggest supporters and advocates. Our very own Empresses!

Take a deep breath in and a deep breath out. Open your eyes. Place your branch in your jar.

❖ Now, fill up your jar with your chosen moon water. We are using new and waxing moon water to help facilitate growth for everything we are cultivating with this spell today.

❖ Once you are done, hold your jar in both hands or hover your hands above it, and say aloud,

> *I call to the energy of the Empress to guide me on this journey.*
> *The one toward self-love and acceptance, of that I am worthy.*
> *I open my heart and my mind toward my true self, my true identity.*
> *From here on forth, with harm to none, so it is and so it shall be.*

❖ Close your jar and place it somewhere on your Empress altar as a reminder to step into your power of love and acceptance each day.

❖ If you called the corners for this spell, close them by going backward through the routine you performed.

❖ I recommend leaving an offering of chocolate for the Empress as thanks!

Journey to Self-Love and Acceptance Divination Spread

Lay these cards out in whatever spread shape works best for you. There is no predetermined layout so you can use the tarot's energy in the way that works best for you.

Card 1—Where you are currently on your journey

Card 2—What is holding you back (blockage)

Card 3—What needs to be faced to overcome this

Card 4—What is guiding you forward

Card 5—How to best continue to utilize this guiding force

Card 6—Why you are worthy of self-love and acceptance

Card 7—Why this journey will be well worth it

Your Body's Altar

We are magick, our bodies are magick—that is what the Empress likes to remind us through the imagery on her card. She teaches us that we have the power to create, grow, and express ourselves in so many different ways just by using our bodies in ways that benefit and feel good to us. So, of course, we can use our bodies as altars and vehicles for magick.

We can access our bodies' altar and the energy of the Empress by utilizing glamour magick in our practices. Glamour magick is often practiced by choosing what goes on our bodies with intention and purpose, such as clothing, jewelry, makeup, body washes, oils. We can also use mirrors magickally for this work.

Different Things to Add to Your Body's Altar

COLORS

Reds—For confidence

Pinks—For self-love

Yellows—For happiness and strength

Black—For personal power and protection

Green—For personal growth

Brown—For grounding

FABRICS

Cashmere—Comfort

Gauze—Healing

Silk(y) and Satin(y)—Sensuality and transformation

Velvet—Confidence and magick

Lace—Sensuality and sexuality

Leather(-like)—Confidence and protection

JEWELRY

Gold—Confidence and happiness

Silver—Beauty and reflection

Citrine—Confidence and happiness

Gold obsidian—Sunshine in ebbs

Labradorite—Revealing true identities

Pyrite—Confidence and self-worth

Red jasper—Confidence and passion

Red tiger's eye—Direction and protection

Rose quartz—Beauty and self-love

PLANT WATER/OIL

Rose—Beauty and protection

Orange—Confidence and happiness

Sandalwood—Ease negativity and sensuality

Cinnamon—Courage and strength[21]

Clove—Sex and sensuality

Rosemary—Resilience and vitality

Jasmine—Beauty and magick

Note on Mirrors

Mirrors are known to be portals of magick, and we can use that to our advantage in glamour magick practices, especially if you are someone who doesn't like cosmetics or oils. Place personal sigils for things like confidence, happiness, protection, sensuality, or strength, with the purpose of reflecting that energy toward not only yourself but for others to see in you, through your body. This can be done in your bathroom mirror or even a compact mirror!

Magickal Things to Do at Your Body's Altar
Empress Body Oil

WHEN TO DO THIS:

- ❖ A full moon in Libra or Taurus
- ❖ A Friday for Venus Day

WHAT YOU WILL NEED:

- ❖ Rosebuds—To help you bloom
- ❖ Saffron—For your sensuality and sexuality
- ❖ Cinnamon stick—For confidence and strength

---

[21] Editor's note: Please note that cinnamon can be harsh on the skin, so use a very small amount and test it before lathering on any cinnamon products. You can also use it on fabrics you're adorning yourself with if you're concerned about this.

- 21 drops of rose essential oil—For inner beauty and self-love
- 15 drops of sandalwood essential oil—Protect against negativity and to aid sensuality
- 9 drops of clove essential oil—To help assert your power and sensuality
- Apricot kernel carrier oil—For self-love, emotional support, and protection
- A 1-ounce vessel for your oil

Add all ingredients into your vessel with intention (remembering why you are adding them, by using the correspondences given). Start with the solid ingredients and then move on to the oils.

I recommend spending time with each of the ingredients to connect with their energy by envisioning their properties manifesting in your life. This deepens your relationship with the plants so you can form connections with them.

When you get to the carrier oil, fill your vessel to the top.

If you are doing this the night of a full moon, leave outside under the moon's rays with a crystal grid of rose quartz and quartz to help amplify the energy of your oil!

I recommend keeping this oil on your Empress altar when it is complete. Use often, especially when you need to feel more confident within yourself, if you are indulging in your sensuality, or if you just want to connect deeper with the Empress.

Empress Meditation

For this meditation, I recommend getting as comfortable as possible. After all, our Empress is an Empress of comfort. This can mean relaxing your body in a comfortable chair, sitting on top of a fluffy pillow, or even lying down on your bed! Whatever resonates with you the most and is the most snug and cozy.

If you want to add to the luxury of this meditation, maybe light some rose incense or spray the area around you with rosewater to help set the mood! Apply some of the Empress body oil. You could also put on some soft instrumental music, brown noise, or singing bowl music. I personally prefer to listen through noise-canceling headphones to help me focus.

When you are ready and are nice and comfortable, close your eyes. Take a deep breath in, filling your whole body with air (not just your upper chest) and a deep breath out, concentrating on releasing it all. Repeat until you feel relaxed and maybe a little fuzzy around the edges.

Envision yourself in a field like the Empress on the card. Hear and see the golden stalks of wheat in front of you to create a gentle shhh-ing sound as the wind travels through them, the emerald waterfall hitting the rocks below, and the trees gently swaying in the background filling the air with a woodsy scent.

You sit on a self-created throne.

You are in your element.

You are in your power.

You are at your most confident and free.

You are free to express yourself however you choose.

(Note if you are sitting up proudly or if you are lounging like a cat in the sun. What symbols do you surround yourself with that proudly display your identities? Are there flags, symbols, or even plants that correspond to them?)

Now you notice there is a painter, painting this scene of you. Travel around to see what they have been working on while you are lounging in the sun. What do you see? How have you been depicted not as the Empress herself, but as your own divine ruler?

When you are ready to return to your body, concentrate on your breathing. Fill your lungs with as much air as can fill them and then release it all. Begin wiggling fingers and toes.

Make sure to write down your experience!

Return to this space to feel empowered whenever you need it.

A LIFE WELL BUILT

Exploring Queer Adulthood with the Minor Arcana

By Cassandra Snow

It is an understatement to say that when I first found tarot I was lost. I was only eighteen years old. I was coming off of a lifetime of codependency and trauma. I was deeply in the closet, and had been so staunchly in the closet for so long that I'd silenced my inner voice well beyond the bounds of my gender and sexuality. In so many ways, I was living a double life then. I was partying with the theatre kids at night and showing up bright and early for church the next day. Yet somehow it never felt like a double life. In fact, it never felt like I was living at all. I was sleepwalking through my own life, going through the motions and then spiraling when I looked at the bottom of my empty cup and didn't see any vision of myself reflected there.

That was twenty years ago.

Today my life would be unrecognizable if not for a couple of grounding mainstays, tarot being near the top of that list. When I started tarot, my life was a never-ending cycle of Death, the Tower, Judgement, and then back to the start with the World. These days I pull Swords cards to remind myself to write and Cups to remind myself that my sister's birthday is coming up. It's not that there are not major things like death, taxes, and trying to become a single gay parent. It's not like my gods don't show up and scream at me to pay attention to them. It's just that I'm privileged enough to not be living in a constant state of emergency anymore. Excitingly, this reliable deck of seventy-eight cards is every bit as important to me as it ever has been.

When you are in survivor mind-set, you are not thinking about a future or even a life. The idea of building one is a completely bizarro world concept. In 2004 it was all I could do to not flunk out of college and risk losing my meal plan (without which I was not likely to eat). I had no concept of futurity. Similarly, I had no real concept of what living out of the closet might be or look like. Everything I saw that could be called representation was from the doom and gloom of the closet. Growing up in the 1990s and early 2000s meant even that gloomy representation was hard to come by. As I was attempting to face so many of my own truths, I had no guiding star to look to that would help me find my way. In fact, the entire time I was coming out of the closet, moving halfway across the country, learning to love, and figuring out how to express myself for real (and not out of trauma-born scarcity), no one told me what happens to a queer person "after" all of the big life-shattering realizations and confessions.

There was a lot of honestly pretty good literature and media about realizing you are a queer person in this time. I thrived in Melissa Etheridge lyrics and saw . . . something . . . in those illicit *Rocky Horror Picture Show* screenings. Yet this was, not to date myself, a few years even before Dan Savage's well-intentioned (if flawed) It Gets Better campaign. There was nothing about building from a truer, healthier place. There was no one to teach me how to build a queer life, day in and day out for the rest of my life. There was not one example provided of what that might look like. No one was there to listen to my anxiety about all of the "then what happens?" fears I was housing.

No one and nothing except, of course, the tarot.

While I was struggling to even want a future, the tarot spoke of it anyway. Eventually, I learned to zoom out and listen, trusting that each card could hold not only the secrets to surviving another day but the secrets to getting past those days too. Now, as I mentioned, my life is almost unrecognizable to my suffering eighteen-year-old self. As a result, I find myself looking to the Minor Arcana, their stories and overlooked but rich layers of art and symbolism, more frequently than I do the Majors these days. I find myself not looking for big existential questions, and it's rare that I'm anticipating a true Tower moment in the personal. Instead, the Minors continue to teach me what queer living can and should look like. More importantly, the Minors continue to teach me what queer living can and should *feel* like and how I can get there.

Wands

Wands cards teach me about fight, fire, and passion. These are big ideas and themes, but they also must be tempered and nurtured in order to sustain. Sometimes you have to feed a fire, and sometimes you have to put it out. This teaches me about energy management. Wands also show the reasons we should work to sustain those flames and how we can do so. The journey from the Ace to the Ten of Wands shows me that love, activism, and art are long games. There is no "end." We burn all out in the Ten; then we rest, find our inner Page, get back up, and stoke those fires all over again. We learn to be grateful in this suit that this is the life we've sought and fought for. We learn to do the work even when it's tedious—but we also learn how to rest, play, and get creative in that tedium.

In my own sexual queerness, Wands show me that sexual pleasure, reciprocated love, and the state of raw creativity I prefer to live in are not only valid but make up a substantial one-fifth of the tarot deck itself. While these cards may show that we are not guaranteed our successes when it comes to these things, they continue to light the way. The Wands urge us toward the knowledge that if we take care of ourselves at each step of the process of living impassioned, we will nurture the fire just enough to keep going. Even if we hit a few speedbumps along the way, the end comes, and our own fire lights the way to it.

The Wands are full of cautionary tales along the way of that impassioned life though. These cards taught me that fire burns, and if she walks in with too much swagger, I should grab my Knightly horse and run off into the sunset with myself. Yet they also taught me that controlled burn heals, over time, and sometimes we need to take out what's rotting so it doesn't spread.

Wands are often tied to gut instinct, to spiritual will, and to our supposed earthbound duty to create. In the mundane, these messages remind to simply listen to my gut. That there is no wrong thing to want, only wrong ways to go about it. That creating something is better than creating nothing. This is all so true in my activism, my art, my writing—all the things that make up my day to day. They are also true to my experiences of queerness itself. Gut instinct does not mean anything but whatever it means for me in that moment. Spiritual will means the will to show people how passion and pleasure can be holy. Earthbound duty to create reminds me that we can build a better world, if we take the step-by-step approach the Minor Arcana prefer.

Here is something the Wands have been whispering to me lately: A wand is not just will, gut instinct, vague concepts. A wand is not raw creativity or potential on its own. A wand is not sexual magnetism itself. A wand is the tool we use to direct all of that power. A wand shows our own hand picking up that tool and focusing our will as a powerful part of our life's equation. Wands say that rock by rock, we can build (if not move) mountains. The Wands tell us that a life well-lived is a life worth hurting for. It's also a life worth learning how and where to direct my energy to create something beautiful for.

The Wands taught me, and continue to teach me, how to build a life in which I fight for the life I want, the world I want, and have a lot of hecking fun in the meantime.

Cups

The Cups take their time and teach me about art—the art I want to create and how to process the art I took in. These cards show me that self-expression is the root of everything beautiful. That my voice matters. That all of the pain and heartache and joy and love that drip off of my voice matters. They taught me that that's true of you too and that when we try to connect over our humanity, it is healing.

The Cups tell me that all kinds of love are valid, whether it queer and sexual, queer and romantic, queer and familial, or simply the love I feel when I am sick and my cat is curled up in my lap trying to purr it all away. The Cups say over, and over, and over again that my life is also who I build this life with. They guided me to the realization that there is no better love than the love we feel for the world, Earth itself and the lifeforms upon it. Acting from that place of global love and hope, we can create the Ten of Cups we want to see reflected everywhere. I know it's true—the Cups showed me how.

The Cups teach me in the here and now how to build a life as an artist and romantic, and how to never back down from all the kinds of art and love I believe in. I often think of Wands as the thing we are attracted to and the attraction itself. Cups are what we do with that attraction—why we pursue some flames and let others fall by the wayside. The Cups show up to remind us that reciprocity and fulfillment are a huge part of why we love but that love itself is a sacred gift.

The Cups teach me that whimsy, play, and imagination are the key to so much more than we realize. They teach me how to tap into those things even (and especially) when I do not want to—how to make the most of the good and bad times. They teach me that the moments of frolicking are what being alive is all about, and how to find meaning, beauty, and joy in everything. Yes, everything.

Like the Wands are not the fire itself, Cups are not just the ideas they introduce and reintroduce us to. They are the vessel holding them too. The Cups are the things and people our hearts desire, but they are also our hearts. They are the people we give pieces of our heart to, for better or worse. They are the art we've made that holds those expressions tight for us, freezing sacredly simple moments in time. Cups are the life we build when we hold tight to the dreams within our hands.

And, Cups are the absolute art that happens when we loosen our hands and let the water swirl and mix together all the colors we so carefully laid out.

Swords

The Swords are our logical brain, and while many people struggle with this suit, I welcome it these days. This is the suit of intellect, communication, and technology. Intellect here does not necessarily mean academia, but simply the parts of life we use our brain for. The Swords taught me that looks different for everyone and that that's okay. You see, they also taught me what "using my brain" looks like for me and how to stand strong in my boundaries around that.

Where the Cups taught me to express myself earnestly, the Swords taught me how to do so kindly and quickly when the situation called for it. These cards taught me all about ripping the Band-Aid off and how to let the air itself do its job from there. When I was twenty-two, boundaries versus kindness were all about figuring out who the heck I even was. Today, they keep me working during work hours so I can play later. They prove to me that the space those boundaries protect allows for the rest of life to breeze in beautifully.

Yet the Swords, as a suit, *do* end unhappily. These cards reflect for me, unfortunately, that sometimes life is just hard. Grief escapes no one. Betrayal, heartbreak, illness—these things happen to even the most well-balanced and privileged among us. These cards show me how to accept those moments and walk through the stages of grief. They show when acceptance often feels like defeat but also like maybe it's okay not to win sometimes. Relatedly, Swords show me when the odds are stacked against me, and when I have privilege in ways that are not universal. They show me where the boundaries others impose become restriction or oppression. They show me how to fight that. How to wield my privilege for good. How to one-up an able-bodied, white supremacist patriarchy when necessary. It is through the Swords that I find the grit and determination to pick up a Sword and fight for myself and others, even if I lose that fight.

The Swords teach me practical, tangible lessons too. This is the suit most likely to show up when Mercury is in retrograde and I've been putting off computer repairs. This card reminds me that tarot is meant to be applied today, and that means the STEM side of our life needs its proper attention too. Like it or not, technical devices are here to stay, and the Swords can show us how to work with them instead of against them.

Every day, the suit of Swords reminds me of the difference between logical thought and overthinking. They reveal all the gray space therein. While it might sound counterintuitive, it is largely the Swords that guide me out of binary thinking and into embracing the plenty that makes up life through these reveals.

Swords are not just communication, intellectual pursuits, and thought—they are the way we weaponize those things for better or worse. Swords are literally weapons, and in that, they can absolutely teach us how to use the modern-day tools at our disposal for good. *And*—they remind us that, especially under our white supremacist cisheteropatriarchy, self-defense and defense of others are not only valid but necessary.

The Cups and Wands guide me in the dreamy, meandering moments of being a professional writer, but the Swords taught me how to write in the practical. These cards have guided my hand when editing my own work and have certainly guided me through work on this essay anthology. This suit knows that technical skill can be repetitive and tiring, but it always makes The Work better in the long run. They showed me how to build that technical skill, and they show me now how to keep learning and growing in it.

The Swords teach me to write, to build a life as a writer. They teach me how to communicate with my loved ones. They teach me how to treat my technology and my medical team. They show me how to let that medical team treat me as a disabled person who relies on them for access and quality of life.

The Swords teach me to remember what I've been through and honor all the former pieces of myself, but like that Knight of Swords, sometimes it's still best to cut and run.

Pentacles

The Pentacles are often assumed to be simply the material suit. That's okay—they've taught me over the years to think of even material pursuits in new and exciting ways. Materia or the correspondences to our spellwork, for example—these are material. The way we root into anywhere that feels like home, that is material. Life's work, finances aside, is certainly material because it is material change we are making and a material legacy we are leaving to this planet when we go. Material greed? Yes, bad. Yet acknowledging the place and necessity of material as a building block for . . . everything? That's a good thing, and it's this suit that taught me that.

That's not to say Pentacles has pushed me away from thinking about money, home, and career. I came from an impoverished background with a mom on SSI (supplemental security income). Pentacles have provided safety for me to work through the trauma of and, now, beyond that reality. Pentacles taught me to use my resources well when they were sparse. They showed me how to give to others more selflessly on weeks the resources are less sparse. This suit taught me that creation without material isn't possible, and sometimes we just have to get creative about what our material resources are.

Pentacles teach of home often as well. They have shown me that home is not simply where the heart is, but where the heart wants to be. That any environment where we can heal and grow is home. That neighborhoods and cities can be more home than a house. That community can be more of a home than a neighborhood.

Pentacles move slow. They build even slower. They taught me that pacing and moderation are worth it to get to that glorious ten. That sustainability is and should be a cornerstone value of building a life today, whether we are focused on Earth and environmentalism (as this suit very much is) or on how to be there for others without burning out entirely. They teach us about teamwork, about one step at a time. They've taught me how much that all adds up to after a while. They taught me that life is often about growth and process, and that anything worth keeping grows slowly and sustainably over time.

A pentacle itself is not like a wand, sword, or cup. It's not a weapon or a vessel. A pentacle is a talisman meant to represent Earth itself. Pentacles as objects are a reminder that all we do comes back here, to our worldly home. What we do with the magic within that talisman is up to us, but it is a self-sustaining magic and evergreen reminder that it simply exists, with or without our influence. We can do incredible things with it, whether we accept that gift or not.

The Pentacles teach me every day to go slow when I need to. They teach me how to maintain heart-centered business, arts, and writing practices when my own ethics and values are key to all of it. This suit gives me the tangible know-how on maintaining a magical home and spreading my magic and resources through my community. They remind me, every day, that these gifts are meant to be reciprocal. I have trouble receiving, but the Pentacles remind me that a gift given from anyone, including and especially the world we live in, is meant to be cherished.

QUEERING THE LICHENS, QUEERING THE CUPS

by Maria Minnis

Lichens are queer things.
—John Wyndham, *Trouble with Lichens*

It's difficult to definitively categorize lichens. These composite organisms are always many things at once, each a symbiotic partnership between a fungi and an alga. They are neither fungi nor plants; they are always both, portraits of the complex biological mutualism that exists across the kingdoms of life.

The concept of biological individuality has puzzled philosophers across disciplines and generations. All we perceive stems from our human perceptions of time, categorizations, facts, projections, and myriad perceptions of "identity." David Andrew Griffiths of the University of Surrey names six biological criteria that define individuality: anatomy, embryology, physiology, immunology, genetics, and evolutionary background.[22] Never are these criteria mutually exclusive.

The authors of *A Symbiotic View of Life: We Have Never Been Individuals* assert that there is no organism that is fully autonomous and

---

22   David Griffith, *Queer Theory for Lichens*.

independent.[23] From this perspective, all living beings are symbiotic mergers of various streams of life. *The Human Microbiome: From Symbiosis to Pathogenesis* says, "The human body itself serves as a scaffold for a multitude of bacteria, archaea, viruses, and eukaryotic microbes that inhabit discrete anatomical niches and outnumber our own somatic and germ cells by an order of magnitude."[24] Microbiological and botanical scientists have long studied symbiosis and, thanks to the invention of the microscope, zoological scientists are now exploring how animals—including humans—are multispecies amalgams. Ecology reveals that sexual relationships and vertical gene transfer are only part of animals' identities. Our bodies are many things at once, and they are never isolated. What might this mean for queerness in societies that prioritize individualism and demand dogged self-reliance?

Every one of the seventy-eight cards has something to say about relationships: with ourselves, with others, with our environments, with the universe. The suit of Cups particularly highlights this topic, illuminating themes of partnerships, emotions, harmony, community service, creative connection, self-care, respect, family, friendships, humanity, sensitivity to external factors, vulnerability, and boundaries. Nobody is an island.

Many associate the Cups with water. All living beings, from tiny lichens to the great blue whale, require water to survive. Water speaks to our infinite interconnectedness. Water connects us all. The fluidity of the Cups flows life into our connections.

Unfortunately, some readers flatten their Cups interpretations when they prioritize heteronormative, cisgender romantic relationships. But we are like lichens: many things at once. For every single societally normative relationship one may see in the Cups, there are many

---

23 Scott Gilbert, Jan Sapp, and Alfred A. Tauber, *A Symbiotic View of Life: We Have Never Been Individuals*.
24 Emiley Eloe-Fadrosh and David Rasko, *The Human Microbiome: From Symbiosis to Pathogenesis*.

more possible depictions and interpretations of self-acceptance, collective unity, acts of service, creative collaboration, reciprocity, empathy for the oppressed, unique family structures, heart healing, community care, acceptance, collective unity, and platonic intimacy. There is ample space for queerness.

Today, more ecological conservationists are replacing fixed, binary categories, such as human versus nature and wild versus domestic, with "queer ecologies." Grace van Deelen of the Sierra Club notes,

> *In recent decades, the traditional environmental movement has come under criticism for its reliance on fixed, binary categories—such as wild versus domestic and human versus nature—to guide conservation work. Those who study how humans interact with the outdoors say this mindset prevents caring for any beings, human or nonhuman, who aren't easily categorized ... Queer ecology (or ecologies, to recognize the many people and cultures involved in this work) aims to break binaries and change how humans interact with the outdoors. ... Queer ecology uses a practice called "queering"—which means, in part, to make something different or strange—to question the assumptions underlying concepts such as "wild" or "natural." Queer ecologists strive toward a world in which human and nonhuman beings are less divided and more entangled and dependent on one another than ever.*[25]

Yes, we are like lichens: many things at once.

Queering the Cups renders the suit more expansive and more representative of the nonbinariness of the natural world, including humans. Our species' survival has been dependent on community and collaboration, and those things come in many forms. We are infinitely complex and interconnected; our uniqueness reveals that there is no single "natural" way to be a human. To survive, we can look to the lichen for

---

25   Grace Van Deelen, *What Is Queer Ecology?*

inspiration: All of us are many things at once, and because we rely on each other, we must take care of each other.

The queer, symbiotic nature of life on earth can reveal our distinctive relations and responsibilities to each other through the Cups themes.

The Ace of Cups represents the full expression and possibilities of the suit. Because we are interdependent, we owe each other opportunities to freely love and connect.

The Two of Cups speaks to introductions, inspirations, and harmony. Because we are interdependent, we owe each other our gifts in order to inspire expression that benefits our wider communities.

The Three of Cups portrays altruism and collaboration. Because we are interdependent, we owe each other the respect of our differences in order to create something bigger than ourselves.

The Four of Cups illustrates patience. Because we are interdependent, we owe each other time and space to grow in order to show up in the world authentically.

The Five of Cups points to disappointment, regrets, and shame. Because we are interdependent, we owe each other reminders that we are always whole, no matter what breaks our hearts.

The Six of Cups elucidates giving and receiving. Because we are interdependent, we owe each other the parts of ourselves that balance and complement others' gifts and offerings.

The Seven of Cups can demonstrate projections. Because we are interdependent, we owe each other our self-awareness so that we remember our uniqueness and don't force each other into conceptual boxes that prevent our ability to see and treat people as expansive beings separate from our biases, flaws, and insecurities.

The Eight of Cups encapsulates emotional and spiritual transformation. Because we are interdependent, we owe each other the freedom to choose our own paths rather than tethering them to our fixations of obligatory reciprocity.

The Nine of Cups exemplifies fulfillment and confidence. Because we are interdependent, we owe each other recognition and praise for our contributions to the greater whole.

The Ten of Cups offers a picture of gratitude and happiness. Because we are interdependent, we owe each other our joy, especially in a world that often seeks to quell our joy for the sake of capitalist progress.

The preponderance of lichens is declining due to climate change, which reflects ways that society prioritizes the individual over our shared planet for which we are all responsible. When we remember that we are many things at once, we can cultivate the matrix of the streams of water that make life possible. Breaking free from white-dominant, heterosexual norms of the individual expands our relationships with everything around us. The suit of Cups reveals us the truth: We need water, we need each other, we need connection. We belong to each other.

PART II

FINDING THE TAROT IN OURSELVES

Introduction

This section of essays is equally unique and thought-provoking, but now we're going to look at what happens after enough time spent doing our personal pathwalking with the tarot. At some point, you and your tarot deck, in so many ways, become a team. You will no longer find yourself consistently searching for yourself in the tarot. Instead, you'll begin feeling the tarot's messages and relevance to your life moving through you. These pieces examine this reciprocal relationship, with the writers taking us deep into their own journeys to see how tarot can function not only as a guide for our life, but as a way for us to process the myriad of spiritual, creative, and liberatory messages that come knocking on our door.

This section is pretty technique heavy, but that does not detract from the awe-striking ways that these writers employ these techniques to create a tarot understanding that is totally radical, totally queer, and totally their own. In many ways, finding queerness in tarot's symbols and methods *is* simply adding your own flavor. These writers have asked themselves what works for them and what doesn't. They've done the research. They've dug deep. Now they become experts themselves, offering ways into the tarot that are both innovative and rooted. They are rooted not only in research of the occult themes at play, but in years of personal experience, tracking and note-taking. They are also rooted in all of the other ways we process information—years studying our other passions, for example, and how those might tie into tarot itself.

As you go through these essays, you'll find a lot of wonderful information. If it resonates with you, take your time with them. Come back to them. I've often found that reflecting on a tarot writing months or years after the first encounter makes it hit in all new ways. You've matured, you've grown, and in some cases you've simply changed your mind. Tarot does that too—and hopefully these writings will help you and the cards grow together.

QUEERING THE QUESTIONS THEMSELVES

By Cassandra Snow

There are a lot of questions many tarot readers will choose not to answer. Many readers don't like reading about people who aren't in the room. Many hate yes or no questions. A lot of readers will grimace if you ask only about specific outcomes. I'm pretty flexible though, so I'm not opposed to much... with one exception. Legally, I will not and can not answer anything you should be asking a doctor, lawyer, or therapist instead. Other than that, I'm happy to provide answers, and I trust my clients to do good with those answers. That doesn't mean I don't understand it when my colleagues have to bite their tongue or work to prevent themselves from rolling their eyes. There are questions that are better than others. Frankly, there are questions that are even bad, IMQO. If asked, I am happy to help a client redirect.

Of course, there are no right or wrong questions when we are talking about queerness, identity, or community. There *are* better questions—questions whose answers will light us on fire, refill our cup, cut to the chase, or help us build something beautiful. There are questions that will help us revel in our own queerness and create a better world in our wake as we walk proudly through it. Just like there are bad questions, there are also good questions. Those are the questions I want to help you learn to ask now.

So what makes a question good? This is an age-old dilemma, and something Siri Vincent Plouff and I spent a lot of time talking about when we were writing *Lessons from the Empress* together. They have a section in that book on asking Magic Questions—that is, questions that lead us to the most specific and interesting information we could get. I didn't want just Siri's and my voices in this section though. In my heart, this has always been a community project. So when I ran into trouble articulating some of my own thoughts around questions, I turned to community—specifically online community. I threw up a question box on my Instagram stories and asked my followers what they thought made good or better questions. Their answers were lovely, and the ones I agreed with most included these:

- ❖ A question is good if you take accountability within it. (Jdeets03)

- ❖ A question becomes good when you release the expectation of an answer. (Hannah Levy, creator of *The Rebis* print magazine)

- ❖ A question you're a little afraid to ask but open to the answer to is a good question. (Lane Smith, author of *78 Acts of Liberation*)

- ❖ I like questions with clear focus and intent behind them. (Amtrak112)

My own answer, like most things, depends on the context. The short, snarky one you'll get if I'm feeling sassy (especially when it comes to tarot) is "whichever questions get you the information you ACTUALLY want or need." In other words, don't beat around the bush. Ask what you actually, really, truly want to know.

If you're not sure what you want to know, then the idea of "good" questions becomes more fluid. I love working with fluid, intangible energy, but a lot of you rightfully will not—especially in the beginning.

It's also not appropriate in every circumstance, just as cold, cool logic is not applicable in every circumstance. In these cases when you *do* want and need some kind of answer that isn't just a pep talk or some flowery words, I suggest asking yourself these four questions:

- How do I feel right now (and why)?
- How do I want to feel instead?
- What information or line of questioning will help me move from A to B?
- Therefore, what do I need to ask the tarot?

You might notice these questions build off each other in a tangible and linear way. That's on purpose—you can absolutely use this as a simple four-card tarot spread, laid out in a straight line. A good question gives you the information you're looking for. A good queer question, then, answers questions you didn't even know you had about authenticity, values, and becoming comfortable in who you are. A good queer question asks why things are the way they are, and if that way works for us. A good queer question asks what we can build or create when there is nothing, or how we can come together as a community when work is already being done. A good queer question creates a better world two ways: in the esoteric, by putting it out there at all, and in the practical, by encouraging you to find answers and solutions.

Take a few moments here and think about your normal line of questioning for the tarot. How can you improve it to get better answers? How can you improve it to get queerer answers? What can you take away from this piece, moving forward, to help you come to the tarot for any reason and leave knowing you can have a positive impact on your own life *and* the world at large?

I know that when we come to the tarot we are very often focused inward. This isn't wrong and, in many ways and situations, it is right. I'm not trying to convince you to turn every question into one of creation or activism. I do think it is a largely shared value among queer people today that we want to do as little harm as possible. Incorporating this value and others also leads to better questions, deconstruction of harmful learned thoughts and behavior, and deeper, truer self-knowledge. These are questions that probe us deeper. The ones that make us think outside the box. These are the questions that help us notice how society's ills are infecting us and that lead us to the salve we need.

Included now are some questions that I, friends, or clients have used to help us really blossom and thrive in ourselves, our bodies, and the world at large. I want to start super internally. The following seven questions are designed to help you get to know yourself better. This is framed around gender and sexuality, but leave space for other messages the cards might fill in for you here.

- *Am I queer?* This question might seem silly, but sometimes the biggest and most obvious questions are the ones we are afraid to ask. As a bonus, this question will also help you frame what queerness means to you and how you move through the world on account of it. These ideas were brought up in the introduction to help us frame how and why we use the tarot cards, but if you got stuck, the tarot itself is absolutely here to help you out.

- *How am I queer?* This is when those pesky cards that we still seem to marry to binary gender or heteronormativity no matter how much unlearning we've done actually come in handy. With questions posed like this, starting with a *how*, the answers can give you guidance on if gender, sexuality, or relationship orientation are where we're finding the start of the blurred edges between what we thought we knew of ourselves and what we actually know.

- Following the former question, you could then ask, *Where is there blur, fluidity, and space for experimentation?*

- *How can I more deeply explore my queerness?*

- *Where am I uncomfortable in my queerness?* Other questions in this lineage might include *what feels unclear, too tight, too sticky right now?* Or, *where is that discomfort or uncertainty coming from?*
- *How can I relate or share my experience of queerness with others?* You can piggyback on this initial question by then asking how sharing those experiences might help you feel more connected to others.
- *What does queerness mean to me right now?*

For a lot of us, queerness is wrapped up in relationship. I don't just mean romantic or sexual relationship here, though certainly that too. Here I am speaking of relationships with the world, with our friends, with community, or with found or chosen family. Relationship can take on a more esoteric meaning here too. It can refer to the queer ways we relate to our bodies or spirit (and how we worship them accordingly). Here are some questions about all of these kinds of relationships that have potential to blow things wide open for you:

- *What can I safely offer others right now?* This one is great because it's such a flexible question. You can substitute the name of a partner or found family member instead of the word *others*, for example. You can swap in various actions or movements that you are connected to. I very often use this wide, vast version of the question if I'm thinking about injustice more broadly. Certainly, though, I have gotten as specific as asking what I can offer my best friend, the homeless encampment down the street, and my sick (now late) cat.
- *What do I need that others could provide right now?*
- *What do I want that others can provide right now?*
- *How can I give back to people or communities that helped me get to [this achievement or point of growth]?*
- *How can this relationship feel best for all involved?*

- *Which relationships am I safest to play and explore my queerness in?*

- *Which side of myself does [person/community/etc] pull to the front?* You can follow this one up with questions like *Am I happy with that dynamic?* and *What do I want to show them that I haven't yet?*

- *How can I create or hold space for those who need it?*

- *What space do I need right now?*

- *What actions will show love to [person/community/movement] right now?*

When I think about my own queerness, of course, I think about everything we've talked about so far. I also think about how my work as a theatre artist, writer, and general creative has been impacted by said queerness. I recall the space queerness and art have given me to frolic and try out some funky stuff. I reflect on the expression this combination has allowed when words or conversations have failed or scared me. Anything you're creating falls under this umbrella. This includes a lot of activist and advocacy work. For many of us, it includes how we build homes and families that queer or openly rebel against the compulsory nuclear family. Think about how many things you are making and how special that is. The following list of questions will help you as you create:

- *What am I creating from scratch?*

- *What am I building on or adding to that others before me created?*

- *What am I building on or adding to that is being created now?*

- With either of the first two questions, I like following up with *How I can honor and respect others in these spaces with me?*

❖ *What have I already created? What are my next steps for that creation?*

❖ *What needs created? Who needs to create it? How can I be a part of it?*

❖ *How is my creation affected by my queerness? What values and perspective am I bringing to the table?*

❖ *How is my queerness impacted by the things I build, how I build them, and who I build them with?*

Obviously, this is the world's smallest sample of questions you could ask in our never-ending quest to queer tarot, the world, and questions themselves. My hope here is not just to give you a list of questions to use in your discovery, though certainly that is something I am more than happy to provide. What I *really* want though is to inspire you to come up with your own questions. I want to see you making your own lists or designing your own spreads. When we meet, I want to talk about how we are both working on our critical thinking + improv skills and how that has allowed us to regularly come up with questions we didn't know we need answered until they came to us in a flash of inspiration. I want you to be in queer conversation with the cards and yourself. And I would love to one day join our conversations together.

I'll end this piece with an invitation, a final question for you to mull over or pull cards about that ties all this together:

We are all trying to make a world that is better, stronger, queerer, more fun, and more aligned with our values. What role does tarot itself play in that for you? How can you maximize the time and energy spent with your seventy-eight new queer friends to make it so?

There aren't wrong answers to that. There are only answers that sell yourself short or cut yourself smaller. Strive instead for questions that allow for expanse. For joy. For lust. For better worlds. Strive for all things queer. All things radical. All things beautiful. All things *you*.

QUEERING TAROT'S NUMBERS

Affectionate Alternate Title -
"Gay Math: I Know, But Listen"

By Meg Jones Wall

Introduction

Math has never been my strong suit. As a curious kid who did not do particularly well in school, I would skip math the most often. These were the classes passed only by the skin of my teeth.

Yet for so many of us who are simultaneously spiritually inclined and mathematics avoidant, numerology offers an accessible, user-friendly path to working with numbers. Rather than dealing with complex calculations or abstract algorithms, numerology taps into the inherent energies within each digit, weaving these patterns into larger stories, cycles, and lessons. Numerology is magical and is more of a language than a science.

Whether we like it or not, numbers are all around us. They serve as building blocks and structures, organizing principles that help us make sense of the worlds around and within us. Often called cosmic or divine code, numbers act as sacred tools of a larger force—weaving magic into the mundane. But much of numerology, especially when utilizing older texts and cultural traditions, is intensely heteronormative. From gendered binaries to very specific ideas of material success, numerology hasn't always left room for those of us at the margins.

Fortunately, we can collectively reclaim numbers through a queer gaze, bring our own experiences and insights into our understanding of each digit, and go beyond traditional viewpoints into something new, something expansive, something transformative. Particularly in the tarot, this kind of discovery-oriented vision can help us identify and utilize existing patterns, cycles, and definitions, collectively developing a queer language that's all our own.

This is not a definitive guide to queer numerology, but a starting place. Your unique viewpoint, your individual perspective, your experiences and insights are essential to the integration of numerology into your tarot practice. How can we as queer people reimagine these digits, go beyond the tired definitions that so often get repeated but not interrogated? What could numerology become when we move beyond binaries and into radically queer ways of thinking?

A Note on "Traditional" Numerology

Numerological concepts can be found in most cultures throughout history, meaning that there are many different schools of thought when it comes to numerology: traditions that span centuries, that ascribe different meanings to different digits. Every number has dozens and dozens of mythologies, stories, insights, discoveries, ideas, fears, superstitions, elements, and beliefs attached to it, meaning that there are no consistent singular definitions for any number—and that for every idea in one culture, there may be a contradictory idea in another.

My own practice is rooted in Pythagorean numerology, developed by the controversial but influential Greek philosopher Pythagoras around 525 BCE. He believed that "numbers have qualities" and are innately spiritual.[26] But Pythagoras also combined multiple schools of thought and disciplines in order to develop his system, borrowing from Arabic, Druid, Phoenician, Egyptian, and Essene sciences,[27] among others, to create meanings that resonated with him.

There is such a wide depth and breadth of numerological meanings from across the centuries that trying to boil down any number to just a few keywords is arrogant at best, and a willful misunderstanding of numerology's history and potential at worst. In other words, we are not doing anything new or profane in making numerological meanings queer, in claiming them as our own. In fact, it could be said that by expanding our concepts of these numbers, we are actually following tradition, rather than flying in the face of it.

The definitions that I will offer here as "traditional" or "commonly accepted" are merely the tip of the iceberg, simply a starting place rather than be-all, end-all interpretations. That's how this works: In order to queer something, we first have to recognize what already exists. It's only then that we can stretch beyond it, and make it something new.[28]

Queering numerology has the potential to be intensely personal. You might not agree with my ideas or suggestions, and that's wonderful—it means that you are already tapping into your own wisdom and that you are forming ideas that are clarifying rather than conformative.

Stay with that energy.

Take notes.

Listen.

Pay attention to what resonates and what doesn't.

This is merely a jumping-off point; you get to chart the course from here.

---

26   Faith Javane and Dusty Bunker, *Numerology and the Divine Triangle* (Para Research, 1979).
27   Hans Decoz, *Numerology: A Complete Guide to Understanding and Using Your Numbers of Destiny* (TarcherPerigee, 2001).
28   Rebecca Scolnick, *The Witch's Book of Numbers: Enhance Your Magic with Numerology* (Hierophant Publishing, 2022); Cassandra Snow, *Queering the Tarot* (Red Wheel/Weiser, 2019).

One // Monad

One, known by Pythagoras as *Monad*, is the source, the origin, the divine. This is primordial and prebiotic, the material that everything else is made from, the beginning of all things, the *yang*. *One* holds endless potential, containing all other numbers, the top and the truth. This is the primal force, the wellspring. Some of the oldest texts define *one* as God the Father, the sum of all wisdom and thought, the origin of everything. Pythagoras didn't work with the number zero, so *one* is the very first number, the start of the cycle, the thing that begins it all and sets all other growth into motion. Without *one*, there can be nothing more.

In the tarot, *one* aligns with the Magician, along with the other *one* archetypes of the Wheel and the Sun, and the Minor Arcana aces and tens. Tarot in general holds a lot of *one* energy, and for good reason: These are initiators and gifts, new ideas or discoveries or realizations or ambitions that light us up, activate our energy, open a door to something different. With tarot *ones*, we explore themes of independence and innovation, activating a new cycle, creating a spark that we hope to nurture into a roaring blaze. *One* is the start, the call, the invitation. And in many sources, both traditional and modern, *one* is considered masculine.

There's something powerful, something magical, something deeply and profoundly beautiful about becoming our own source. With these more traditional interpretations and modern lenses, *one* becomes something outside of ourselves, something that initiates, something that activates or shows up to inspire us. If *one* is divine, and we are human, aren't we too different to alchemize? When we queer this first digit, we empower ourselves to chart our own paths forward, to invent or reinvent ourselves in our own image, to honor the divinity that already lives within us. Whether you believe in many gods, one god, no gods, or something else entirely, *one* is all about tapping into our own creativity, blazing trails, opening doors, and expanding our perspective on what we previously thought was true.

One challenges, *one* innovates, *one* liberates. *One* gives us permission to reimagine something, or everything. *One* pushes and inspires, strategizes and daydreams, experiments and prepares. Queering *one* is giving ourselves permission to think beyond the binary, beyond the black and white, beyond the rules and restrictions that others have instituted. *One* can be so much more than simply choosing unexpected colors to fill in the lines we see; instead, *one* can be drawing new lines, coloring outside the lines, or selecting an entirely different medium, dismissing the concept of lines altogether.

What are you ready to acknowledge and authenticate? How can you reimagine yourself, and what would it look like to trust in your own capacity for reinvention? What could you give yourself permission to embody, to explore, to express? What would it mean to be your own biggest source of inspiration, to pursue becoming your deepest and truest self?

What if you claimed your ideas, sparks, desires, and impulses as both human and divine?

Two // Dyad

After *one* comes *two*. And where *one* is the source, *two* is the other, the attraction, the duality. *Two* represents opposites and oppositions, the pairs of things that divide and magnetize, the *yin* to the *one*'s *yang*. Good and evil, light and dark, positive and negative—these pairings separate and clarify, defining one by virtue of another. In the same way, *dyad* speaks to casting a reflection, inverting and refracting, the opposite of unity. With traditional notions of numerology, *two* incorporates themes of contrast and knowledge, awareness and discovery, subtlety and passivity. Because of traditional or conservative concepts around the divine and creation, *two* is often associated with feminine energy, and not in a particularly complimentary way; this is the temptation, the enticement, the serpent that causes us to stumble. Unlike *one*'s masculine source, traditional *two* becomes the feminine other.

Within the tarot, cards with this digit can be quiet, hard-to-parse archetypes that are difficult to define, existing in liminal spaces and perhaps frightening or unsettling us with their elusive, ever-changing energy. The Priestess is a figure of patient choice and inner wisdom, of intuition and evaluation. And our other *two* archetypes, Justice and Judgement, along with the Minor Arcana *twos* and the court pages, hold many layers of meaning, often centered around balance, equality, harmony, choice, and emotion. Tarot *twos* see us struggling to figure something out, to choose a path forward, to balance what we know with what we feel.

But I think that we can do better, go deeper, be less heteronormative about all of this. When we queer the number *two*, we embrace not only the duality of the worlds we live in, the endless contradictions in our daily lives, but also the duality that lives within us. We acknowledge the ways that we allow ourselves to shift and grow in different places and at different paces, the various aspects of self that emerge when we feel safe and celebrated versus when we have to be on our guard. We honor our own capacity for safety and self-protection, even as we also delight in the places where we can be fully ourselves, the people who see all of us.

With *two*, we trust in our proficiency for self-discovery and self-knowledge and delight in the magic that we carry. Perhaps we're not like everyone else. Perhaps we even long to be different than we are. But with *two*, we show ourselves empathy, forgive ourselves for moments when we had to hide, acknowledge who we are internally even when we cannot be our full selves externally. If *one* is finding confidence in our own talent for magic and creation, *two* is recognizing the deeper meanings within those sparks, finding the power that allows the sparks to catch into flame.

What do we receive, and where does that come from? How do we trust our own intuition, in a world that sees our identities as false or offensive, that vilifies us for simply wanting to be ourselves? What are we learning about ourselves, based on our choices and our desires?

And what does it mean to hold as much space as necessary for the things that we long for, the things that we naturally gravitate toward?

Three // Triad

After the source, after the duality, we find *three*: what Pythagoras calls the Holy Trinity, the many faces of God, the most profound expression of love. *Three* and the *triad* are creativity incarnate, narrative and story, something coming into being. Where *one* is a point and *two* is a line of connection between points, in combining them the resulting *three* allows us to make a triangle, a tripod, something that can stand on its own. With *three*, we can tell a complete story, observe a pattern, recognize a trio of important ideas that support one another through their intersections and differences.

Especially in the *threes* of the tarot, the Empress along with the Hanged One, the World, and the Minor Arcana threes and knights, we see ideas beginning to be made manifest: coming into the world, taking shape, and having an impact. Creation, expression, and connection are all associated with this number in the tarot, experimenting and taking chances, desires finding their form. And while I tend to shy away from strict gender binaries, it's worth noting that for many traditional tarot scholars, seeing the *one* as masculine and the *two* as feminine leads to *three* as a result of their union, in the form of a child. More simply, we can view this as a creation that is born from collaboration, something that takes multiple voices or energies to come into being.

In queering the number *three*, I tend to think about the spaces where we can fully and authentically express ourselves: the chosen families, the broader communities, and the collectives of folks who align with our values and support our ongoing evolutions. As queer people, we are familiar with making discoveries about ourselves, with seeing something taking shape and finding the truth of it through that process. In being brave enough to speak an idea into being, in letting others witness and hold space for our identity, we find new courage, new confidence, and new magic. *Three* holds the capacity for playful, joyful, honest exploration, for sharing who we are with those who will celebrate us completely, and for finding the strength to tell our real stories.

What do you learn about yourself when you don't have to censor your outpourings and offerings? What do you discover in allowing something to find definition and shape in the world, in letting an aspect of yourself be witnessed? How often do you celebrate the magic that comes forward during play, during experiments, during authentic moments of connection?

What emerges when someone holds space for your truths and your fears?

Four // Tetrad

Now that ideas are starting to come into being, *four* represents the next stage of development: solid matter, roots and foundations, directions and points and corners that help us find our footing. If *one* is the initial idea, *two* is the seed being planted, and *three* is visible growth, *four* (or the *tetrad*) represents a mature and developed product.[29] With *four*, we find structures and containers, boundaries and limits, a number that protects and preserves. Pythagoras took this a step further, aligning the *tetrad* with the spoken word of God, a symbol of immortality.

These ideas are echoed in the fours of the tarot, most notably with the Emperor and the Minor Arcana fours but also seen in Death and

---

29 Shirley Blackwell Lawrence, *The Big Book of Numerology: The Hidden Meaning of Numbers and Letters* (Weiser Books, 2019).

the Minor Arcana queens. These are protectors and rulers, controlled energies that define and clarify. *Four* cards are dependable, reliable, and stable, bringing a rational and pragmatic energy to whatever they do—not necessarily needing to lead, but able to hold necessary space and delegate to accomplish goals for the greater good.[30] While *three* can be wild, playful, or scattered, *four* offers discipline, focus, and long-term definition.

While these cards can be uncomfortable, *four* creates a lot of space for creating new pathways, systems, and structures that support the vision we hold and the world we want to create. It's all well and good to say that we want something to be different, but without long-term ambitions and without organization and collaboration and leadership, changes cannot be sustained in a lasting way. In queering *four*, we take back the power from capitalist systems and the deeply ingrained beliefs of white supremacy and define our own world.

We all deserve safety, protection, boundaries that support, rules that define and clarify. When we create spaces that are stable, it allows for bigger dreams, deeper vulnerability, more profound connections. As queer people, we can't be afraid of leadership, of power, of strength. We simply have to be intentional about wielding it, about creating checks and balances that actually function, about building in ways to ensure that all voices are heard and held.

How does safety create deeper opportunities for collaboration, sensitivity, creativity, and innovation? What kinds of ideas or ideals are you building upon? Which morals, beliefs, limits, support systems, rules, and experiences stabilize and reinforce your own work, rest, solitude, connections, and dreams? What boundaries have you set that help you find new kinds of freedom and opportunities for growth?

What would it look like to unapologetically take power for yourself and create systems that will enable intentional evolution?

---

30 Maria Minnis, *Tarot for the Hard Work: An Archetypal Journey to Confront Racism and Inspire Collective Healing* (Weiser Books, 2024).

Five // Pentad

Having reached the middle of the number sequence, we find *five*, the *pentad*, an important moment of decision. Traditional sources associate *five* with equilibrium, balance between celestial or spiritual meaning and bestial, primal, deeply human instinct. The *pentad*, or pentacle, can represent humanity or marriage, balance or elements or protection, among other things. But as this symbol includes overlapping lines and sharp angles, it's also associated with destruction, a lack of coherence, or the elimination of what is no longer useful.[31]

The Hierophant is a complex figure, but tarot fives also include Temperance, the Minor Arcana fives, and the court kings. These are cards of breakthroughs and struggle, of obstacles and friction, of integrating what we have known into what we are now pursuing. There is often discomfort associated with fives, a dawning awareness of conflict, a transformative experience that may require us to leave the old behind for the new. *Five* is the number of exchanges, of revolutions, of transition. But in tarot, these cards tend to be associated more specifically with fear, grief, or difficult change, reflecting discomfort around major shifts and a desire for control.

Modern numerology and tarot experts talk about *five* as a number of adventure, freedom, travel, adaptability, and restlessness. In queering the number *five*, I see this as both an acknowledgment of internal friction or cravings and the willingness to shake something up that is holding us back. *Five* has the capacity to help us integrate our own contradictions, to acknowledge, celebrate, and even find power in the aspects of us that don't necessarily make logical sense but work all the same. In being willing to own our mistakes and our learning curves, and in moving through challenges with clear-eyed awareness of our own faults, we have the potential for true growth.

Embracing our queerness, our difference, requires courage. Even if we aren't able to be out everywhere, even if we continue to make new

---

31 Blackwell Lawrence, *The Big Book of Numerology*.

discoveries about ourselves, even if our labels shift and change, queerness itself is radical, transformative, and adventurous. *Five* feels like an inherently queer number to me already: pushing the status quo to something new, changing our perspective on what things and people have the potential to be.

How often do you take risks? What are moments in your life when you decided to try something new, to leave an old path behind, to set a boundary or make a shift that transformed you? Where do your beliefs or ideals or desires contradict one another, and how can you find pleasure and delight in that rather than feeling frustrated by it? What makes sense to you that you can't necessarily explain?

How do your unique contradictions shape your unique perspective?

Six // Hexad

Considered a sacred and perfect number, *six* was called the *form of forms* by Pythagoras, who viewed the *hexad* as a source of harmony. *Six* is traditionally and commonly associated with marriage, unions, and families, with symmetry and balance, with beauty and radiance. As *six* is the doubling of *three*, some texts refer to this as the Christ Force, or a double Trinity: God as well as the reflection of God.[32]

If *five* is destruction or change, *six* is the calm after the storm, a balancing and stabilizing force following upheaval. We see these themes reflected in the sixes of the tarot: the Lovers and the Minor Arcana sixes, as well as the Devil. *Six* is nourishment and expansion, reciprocity, and transitioning away from challenges; and no matter where we may find ourselves on the other side of friction, *six* seeks harmony, for better or worse. These cards associated with *six* are often about recovery, reconciliation, and hope for the future; honoring what we have endured and looking forward with optimism; trying to take control after feeling restless or moving through a complicated period of instability.

---

32 Blackwell Lawrence, *The Big Book of Numerology*.

Queering the number *six* feels first like a natural shift away from heteronormative concepts of marriage and family and toward embracing chosen family, local collectives, unconventional relationship formats, and the communities that have our back through thick and thin. *Six* is pride, celebrating how far we've come, and looking ahead to the progress that we still must work toward. I also see *six* as a number of mutual aid, of showing up for those who need help or support or encouragement, for the marginalized and the overlooked and the systematically silenced. When we queer *six*, we reimagine the family unit as something more expansive, and dream big about the world that we could have if we put our magic together and let it become something bigger and grander and bolder than we ever thought possible.

What does it look like to celebrate on the other side of struggle? How do we find beauty and power in the ways that we are different, in the various skills and talents that others in our community might possess and utilize? What have we learned through transformation and friction, and how do those experiences shape our perspective on safety or stability? What does it feel like to be vulnerable with those we trust, to let them support us when we're struggling or to show up for them when we have the capacity to serve? How do we show up for other people?

What does love in action look like?

Seven // Heptad

While *six* is often tied to physical embodiment and stability, *seven* (or *heptad*) explores the intersection between body and soul. *Seven* is a deeply spiritual number, a sacred digit associated with life, enlightenment, vibrations, and illumination. Regardless of your theology, *seven* is commonly associated with solitude, philosophy, analysis, and a craving for knowledge. This is the esoteric, the hard-to-define, the elusive. This is the mystery that lives within the physical, the hidden and unknowable facets of self and the universe.

As archetype *seven*, the Chariot can be a complicated card in that there are many different meanings and perspectives on it. But through the lens of the number *seven*, and in considering other seven cards like the Tower and Minor Arcana, we can bring this energy into sharper focus. These cards are tied to seeking and finding, wisdom and discovery, navigating internal and external obstacles, and figuring out the purpose that drives us forward. Sevens in the tarot are disciplined and inquisitive, methodically pushing beyond comfort zones and questioning what is on the surface. *Seven* wants to *know*, even if that knowledge leads to disruption, change, or anxiety.

Seven is often about challenging norms, or the status quo, about wanting to understand why something happens and potentially forcing a move in another direction. And in queering this number, there's potential for interrogating both the self and the patriarchal systems that we live in: asking for more, for better, for different. There is risk from interrogating, because sometimes we see or learn things that we don't like, or that make other people angry. It requires a lot of courage to challenge systems or to peer behind the curtain, to dig into uncomfortable truths, to stand firm in our own beliefs.

Yet if we want to truly understand, if we want our world to support all of our many facets and layers and differences, we have to be willing to do this scary work, to push back. When we know what matters to us, we understand what is worth fighting for. *Seven* is about working toward a collective vision for the future that reflects our own deepest values, even if that requires changes, fights, or dramatic shifts in movement.

What is working for you, and what isn't? What do you believe in, and how do those beliefs show up in your work, your play, your relationships with others, your relationship with yourself? How do you stand up for what you believe in, even if you have to stand alone? What are the common threads that are woven throughout your personality, desires, fears, and ambitions?

Which threads hold you together, and how willing are you to examine those threads with care?

Eight // Octad

Referred to in traditional texts as a double mirror that can see the physical and metaphysical worlds simultaneously, *eight* and the *octad* are associated with divine and material power, wealth that is both tangible and intangible. We see here stories of infinity and flow, unrestricted movement and powerful growth, harmony, and balance. There's an ambition and a steadfastness to the number *eight*, cyclical themes of orbits and octaves, moving upward and onward, of having everything we need to succeed. *Eight* has drive, perseverance, and an ability to see something through no matter what it takes.

Similarly, eights in the tarot are associated with power and passion. Strength and the Star are both tied to long-term vision, patience, and endurance. The Minor Arcana eights often encourage us to move forward with courage, to trust in our resources, and to respect the process. Eights can be challenging, because they push us to believe in what we cannot fully see, to be devoted to an outcome that is not yet within our grasp. Still, eights can teach us the power of resilience—not by pressuring us to "be strong no matter what," but instead by encouraging us to slow down, be patient, and practice moderation when necessary. Power can take many forms.

Authentic confidence is not always easy to access. For many folks, power, stability, and success can feel out of reach or hard to come by. But in queering the number *eight*, we look not only to the resources that we hold within us, but the resources that are around us. *Eight* can encourage us to recognize, celebrate, and access the assets that we have at our disposal—through systems, through communities, and through sometimes unexpected means. In being brave enough to ask for what we need, in pursuing something with devotion, in keeping our vision for the future clearly in our sights, we can accomplish so much. With the number *eight*, we believe in ourselves, even if the road is rocky. Through *eight*, we devote ourselves to what matters and let the magic that dwells within us become impossible to ignore.

What does power actually look like, feel like, accomplish? How do we pace ourselves and delegate, rather than burning out by taking on too much? How often do we let ourselves be seen, shine brightly, step up into leadership roles? When is there strength in vulnerability, in asking for support, in letting others cheer us on or even take over when necessary?

What does it mean to be resilient, and how can we challenge our notions of being too self-sufficient to allow others to participate in communal victories?

Nine // Ennead

The final number in the spiral or cycle, *nine* is a number of the horizon, of all we can see, of returning to the self.[33] It's also called the number of initiations, directing our attention not only to the cycle that is concluding, but the fresh start hovering on the horizon. *Nine* represents endings and change, perfecting and completing, generations and awakenings. If *one* is the fully physical person, *nine* is the fully spiritual person, and these two entities can have trouble truly perceiving each other. In this way, traditional sources consider *nine* the most complex or difficult number to grasp.

In the same way, the *nine* cards of the tarot can be multifaceted. The Hermit and the Moon, along with the Minor Arcana nines, are about liminal spaces and transitions, self-knowledge, release, and giving back. There's a lot of compassion woven into these cards, an empathy for self and for others that can show up in philanthropic gifts, holding space, sharing knowledge, and serving as an observant and generous guide for others. All of these cards see us balancing on a precipice, preparing to

---

[33] Blackwell Lawrence, *The Big Book of Numerology*.

shift into a new beginning, and releasing the cycle or story that is concluding. These are often solitary cards, spaces of shadow and retreat, but these cards also have a wide and deep impact on the communities and collectives that they are tied to. *Nine* is influential, lighting a lamp that illuminates the path for others, that will burn in the darkness even after we are gone.

In queering the number *nine*, we are conscious of how what we do impacts others, paves a new way forward, and leaves a lasting legacy. Sometimes it feels like, as queer folks, we have to live in a necessarily protective and isolating bubble in order to survive and thrive—and as legislation around queer and trans communities continues to deny us personhood and autonomy, that can be a reality that keeps us safe, protected, and able to continue living with dignity as much as possible. But when we allow ourselves to be visible, when we are not afraid to go at our own pace and chase our own dreams, when we take actionable steps to create important and necessary change, we also open the door for others who may follow in our footsteps. And when we trust completely in our own process, when we let ourselves be seen for exactly who we are and what we dream of, that process can have powerful ripple effects that we don't even see, ones that last far beyond what we consciously share.

Nine can teach us to let go of the fears, beliefs, anxieties, or indecisiveness that may be holding us back, and instead empower us to follow our own north star, wherever it may lead us. This letting go might require forgiving ourselves for any stumbles along the way, teaching us to cherish our own authenticity, and learning from all that we have endured.

What does it mean to awaken to self, to learn to see ourselves through a clear and generous gaze? How do the things that we do impact those around us, perhaps even serving as a legacy that endures after we're gone? Which daily actions and parts of your routine contribute to broader change? When are you conscious of something ending, of a new beginning ahead?

What are you willing to release, and which possibilities might that release open up for your future?

Final Thoughts

As you incorporate numerology into your own tarot practice, either for the first time or as part of an ongoing methodology, it's my fervent hope that you will take what I've started here and make it your own. Engage with these digits honestly, openly, with curiosity and potential. Look at these numbered groupings of cards together, and meditate on their commonalities and differences, on the ways that each set of cards explores various facets of each number. Let them sing to you, tell you their stories, weave their magic around and within you.

And as you allow the numbers to share their queer authenticity with you, be open to whatever you may find. These digits are complex and layered, but also powerful in their simplicity. You are allowed to make their meanings your own, to adapt them as needed, to read between the lines or toss the lines out the window. How does each digit activate different emotions, different ideas, different memories within you? What does each number offer? And in mapping these numbers into the tarot, how do these discoveries help you create more personal connections with the cards and archetypes?

A SECRET THIRD THING

Court Cards as Queer Elements

by Charlie Claire Burgess

The court cards are notoriously challenging for tarot learners to crack, but for queer readers and querents, they can present an extra layer of difficulty. The gendered titles can make connecting with the court cards uncomfortable or even dysphoric for transgender, nonbinary, genderqueer people, or others who may not fit into the gender binary. The common interpretations in which Kings are rational leaders and Queens emotional caregivers only reinforce stereotypical binary gender norms. The King-Queen pairing itself is heteronormative. The feudal hierarchy with King at the top and Page, traditionally considered a "feminine" card, at the bottom is patriarchal. The most common alternative to the feudal titles is Daughter/Son/Mother/Father, but that only reinforces patriarchy and heterosexism, with an extra heaping of traditional nuclear family values on top.[34] Even if we can successfully parse through all of this, the classic court card problem remains: Do these cards represent actual people in our lives or parts of ourselves? Or something else entirely?

---

34   Many queer readers, authors, and deck creators have tackled the naming issue by renaming the court cards with nongendered and nonhierarchical titles. In my book *Radical Tarot* (Hay House, 2023), I suggest Student, Seeker, Sage, and Steward for Page, Knight, Queen, and King, respectively.

A solution may lie in an already well-established method of reading the court cards, one that is ripe with queer possibilities that have remained mostly unexplored: reading the court cards as elemental energies. The usual way of doing this involves assigning one of the four classical elements of Earth, Fire, Water, and Air to the four court cards of Page, Knight, Queen, and King, thus creating an elemental pairing of card and suit. For example, if we assign water to Queens, the Queen of Pentacles (the suit of earth) would then be Water of Earth. In the standard way of using this method, the elements are interpreted as separate and distinct elemental energies: the Queen of Pentacles would approach the *earth* suit of the material realm in a *water* way that prioritizes emotional and intuitive awareness. All by itself, this method offers a nongendered modality for relating to the court cards . . . but I think we can get even queerer. Here, we will consider the court cards not as sets of separate elements but as queer couplings, trans forms, and nonbinary embodiments of entirely new *queer elements*.

This treatment of the court cards as queer elements is built upon Lee Harrington's concept of "interstitial"—meaning "in between"—elements as articulated in his essay "Queer Elements: Working with Interstitial Energies." Harrington defines interstitial elements as those that fall between the four classical elements of Earth, Air, Water, and Fire. Interstitial elements, they write, "are those that combine elements in such a way as to not know where one starts and the other begins . . . that fall outside of the dyads, outside of the opposites of perceived polarities. They are the queer elements."[35] Harrington explores interstitial elements as corresponding to the intercardinal directions (northeast, southeast, southwest, northwest) in magical practice, but these queer elements can also be applied to the tarot's court cards, opening exciting new possibilities for queer connections and emergent interpretations.

---

35   Lee Harrington, "Queer Elements: Working with Interstitial Energies," in *Queer Magic: Power Beyond Boundaries*, eds. Lee Harrington and Tai Fenix Kulystin (Mystic Productions Press, 2018), 303–12.

Before we can dive into these interstitial energies, we must first introduce the classical elements and consider why they offer particularly resonant avenues for interpreting the court cards.

A Queerly Embodied Court

It is well established that the Minor Arcana suits correspond to the four classical elements of Earth, Air, Fire, and Water. Though there is some disagreement, the correspondences are generally held to be Wands as Fire, Cups as Water, Swords as Air, and Pentacles as Earth, with the Major Arcana corresponding to the mystical fifth element of Aether, or Spirit.[36] When it comes to assigning elements to the court cards, a bit more disagreement exists. According to the Hermetic Order of the Golden Dawn (the 19th-century British magical society that heavily influenced the Rider Waite Smith Tarot and the Thoth Tarot), Pages are Earth, Knights are Air, Queens are Water, and Kings are Fire. The main alternative to this school of thought flips the elemental correspondence of Knight and King, with Knights as Fire and Kings as Air, while the Page and Queen correspondences usually remain the same.

We won't get into the esoteric arguments for and against the Knight/King correspondences here because they are outside the purview of this essay, and because they're somewhat beside the point in the interests of developing a queerer tarot. *The elements you assign to the cards should be the ones that make sense to you, not the ones that the most people agree on, nor the ones that a century-old secret society decided were true.* Being queer, we know that consensus doesn't always correspond to fact, and norms are just another arm of the status quo. Besides, the reasoning for the Golden Dawn's elemental

---

[36] Some readers flip the elemental correspondence for Wands and Swords, with Wands as Air and Swords as Fire. Cups as Water and Pentacles as Earth are uncontested, to my knowledge.

correspondences is based in a hierarchy of elements, and we are not only interested in a queer tarot, but a nonhierarchical one.[37]

Here, I'll use the correspondences that (currently) feel true to me as illustrations, which are Page as Earth, Knight as Fire, Queen as Water, and King as Air. Please use the correspondences that feel right to you.

	Pentacles (Earth)	Wands (Fire)	Cups (Water)	Swords (Air)
Page (Earth)	Earth-Earth	Earth-Fire	Earth-Water	Earth-Air
Knight (Fire)	Fire-Earth	Fire-Fire	Fire-Water	Fire-Air
Queen (Water)	Water-Earth	Water-Fire	Water-Water	Water-Air
King (Air)	Air-Earth	Air-Fire	Air-Water	Air-Air

Table 1: Court Card Elemental Pairs

Assigning elements to the four court cards creates a crosshatch of energies, an intersection and combination of two elements embodied in each card (or, in four cases, one element, doubled). The Page of Wands, for example, becomes Earth (Page) of Fire (Wands). "Earth of Fire" may seem just as confusing as "Page of Wands," but if you spend some time contemplating the energies of the elements, they swiftly become much more intuitive, relatable, and expansive than the obscure offices of Page, Knight, Queen, and King. You might not have a good understanding of what a Page is, but I bet you know what earth is. No matter who we are, what identities we claim, or what cultures we come from, we all know fire, water, air, and earth. This is not to suggest that the way we relate to the elements or their significance across cultures is universal—it's not. Rather, we each know how it feels to drink a glass of water, to touch earth, to breathe air, to feel the heat of a flame. Each of us holds the elements inside of us:

❖ The air in our lungs and our speech

---

[37] For those who must know, according to the Golden Dawn, Fire, as the element closest to the divine in Hermetic Qabalah, corresponds to the divinely appointed King; while Earth, as the basest and most material element, corresponds to the lowliest rank of Page.

- ❖ The fire of metabolism and body heat
- ❖ The water in our blood, tears, saliva, and other body fluids
- ❖ The good earth of our flesh and bones that are made from the very same stuff as the soil and the leaf

The elements are somatic and intuitive. We can each bring our own cultural associations and experiential knowledge to the elements, and this only makes them more personal and resonant for the individual practitioner.

Working with the court cards as elements is intrinsically antihierarchical. Despite the elemental rankings of some esoteric systems, when we consider nature itself, we understand that no element is superior or inferior to any other. Fire may burn the forests, but the earth remains and its soil is nourished by it. Water may drown fire, but fire can also change the form of water through evaporation or melting. Air may seem ubiquitous and untouchable, but air is moved into currents and jet streams by the heat of the sun's fire, the coolness of the ocean's water, and the rotation of the Earth itself. Earth may stand with seemingly eternal permanence, but its surface is shaped by the erosion of wind and water and its very belly is molten fire. There is no hierarchy of elements, only a queer dance of interconnection, interaction, and relationality.

Moreover, working with the court cards as elements instead of people or social roles quite literally takes sex and gender out of the equation, freeing the cards to be interpreted in whatever way feels right to the practitioner regardless of identity. Though occultists have traditionally assigned masculinity or femininity to the elements (declaring nongendered things to be gendered seems to be one of their favorite pastimes), we know that fire, water, air, and earth have no genders. Or maybe they have *all* genders, of which there are far more than two. Either way, reducing them to a false anthropomorphic binary is ridiculous when you spare it a moment of thought.[38] Working with the court cards as elements instead of roles also queers the cards in relation to what it means to be *human*, introducing us to an expansive and more-than-human interpretive approach that is not based on gender, role, or rank but on a deeply felt relationship with queer elemental energies.

Contemplating how fire can be watery or air can be earthy expands our understanding of the classical elements and queers them in relation to their previously fixed and supposedly polar identities. We can go a step further and consider these elements not as simple combinations of fire plus air, earth plus water, but as new elements altogether, ones that have their own energies similar to but distinct from the classical elements: Fire-Air, Earth-Water. These interstitial elements are not only queer elements, they're nonbinary ones. They defy the supposedly polar nature of the elements and collapse the distance between them. They mix and dance in a queer combination and synthesis. They are simultaneously both things and something else entirely, some secret third thing: steam, cloud, lightning, mud, magma, smoke. These elements combine, change, transition, transform. These elements are trans.

The sixteen court cards can be interpreted as energetic expressions of ten elements (see Table 1).[39]

❖ Four are doublings or enhancements of the four classical elements themselves: Fire-Fire, Earth-Earth, Air-Air, Water-Water

---

38   I refer to the gender binary as anthropomorphic because it is a purely human invention that we have based on a flawed understanding of human sexual characteristics (there are far more than two sexes in humans) that we then extrapolated into compulsory behaviors and roles (i.e., gender) and then applied to the entirety of nature, metaphysics, and even divinity. Though we may call the parts of a flower "masculine" and "feminine," they are anything but. If nature shows us anything, it's that existence is far queerer than any of us can conceive.

39   The number *ten* is a meaningful number in tarot. There are ten numbered cards in each Minor Arcana suit, and tarot numerology reduces Major Arcana cards to a number *one* through *nine*, with *ten* signifying the cycle, completion, and return to *one*. *Ten* illustrates unity in diversity and wholeness in division. In the scope of the elements, we may take this to symbolically illustrate the elements—classical and interstitial—as energetic refractions of one cosmic whole.

❖ Six are the interstitial elements of Earth-Air, Air-Fire, Fire-Water, Water-Earth, Earth-Fire, and Fire-Water

Each of the interstitial elements corresponds to two court cards that have the same elemental pairing, but reversed. For example, the Page of Cups (Earth of Water) and Queen of Pentacles (Water of Earth) will both fall under Water-Earth.[40] This is not to say the inverse elemental pairs will express themselves identically, but rather that they will each embody a range of queer Water-Earth (to use the previous example) energies. Exactly how they do that is entirely up to your own interpretation.

Next, I explore the forms and energies of the elements from my own perspective, but I encourage you to do your own contemplation and exploration. Remember, the correspondence for each court card is not definitive. The cards listed under each element are provided for reference based on the correspondences I use. Feel free to mark them out and write in your own.

The Classical Elements

Earth: The Material Realm

PENTACLES, PAGES, PAGE OF PENTACLES

Earth is the element of the material world. Earth is the geometrical perfection of crystals and the mycelial intelligence of mushrooms. It is the craggy starkness of the mountain peak and the rich humus of the forest floor. Earth is fundamental, lush, solid, fertile; it is the foundation we build everything else upon. It is the soil we till and the fruits of that soil that nourish us. Earth is the realm of resources, including natural resources, human resources, and finances. It is also the realm of work and skill, speaking to our bodies and the labor of our bodies, the

---

[40] The order of each queer elemental pairing listed hereafter can just as easily be flipped. Earth-Water is also Water-Earth, and so on. The element named first is not meant to imply dominance or hierarchy.

work we do in the world, and the contribution we leave behind when we're gone. Earth is our first ancestor, our lineage, and our legacy. Earth teaches us about practicality, resourcefulness, sustainability, generativity, and growth.

Air: The Mental Realm
SWORDS, KINGS, KING OF SWORDS

Air is the element of the mind, perception, and communication. It's the crystal-clear view from an eagle's height, the howling gale that levels houses, and the refreshing breeze on a hot summer day. The quality of the air determines if we can see for miles or only a few feet in front of our faces, just as our perception and discernment can be clear or confused. Air is our breath, our scream, and our song. Air is shaped by our mouths and moved across our vocal cords to create speech, aligning the element with communication. Air is also the element of the mind. Like thoughts, air can be tranquil, turbulent, changeable, swift, howling, or stagnant. Also like thoughts, air is not tangible. We cannot grab the air in our hand, but it nonetheless is here and with us all the time—at least in environments where humans can survive. We will eventually die without water, earth (food), and fire (warmth), but being deprived of air will kill us fastest of all. Air is as necessary as it is subtle, as changeable as it is powerful.

Fire: The Energetic Realm
WANDS, KNIGHTS, KNIGHT OF WANDS

Fire is the element of energy, desire, and action. It is the spark of desire that initiates any new endeavor and the heat of purpose that drives its progress. Fire's heat and hunger can be expressed through lust, ambition, passion, or aggression. It can be the steady blaze of a lifetime of activism, the flareup of righteous anger, or the combustion of violence. Fire is creative, inspirational, and transformative. Its shape changes constantly, dancing, leaping, flickering. It's the only element that never stands still. Fire has a spiritual quality that connects us to the divine of our understanding. We can observe this in fire's ceremonial uses: prayer candles, spell candles, novenas, menorahs. Fire can be gentle and supportive: the lamp that lights the night, the hearth fire that warms the house and cooks the food. It can also be all-consuming and destructive if it gets out of hand. As the sun, fire warms the earth, feeds the plants, and makes life possible, but it can just as easily parch, scorch, and burn.

Water: The Emotional Realm
CUPS, QUEENS, QUEEN OF CUPS

Water is the trickling stream and raging river, crashing waves and sucking riptides, quenching rain and crushing ocean depths. Water can be clear and tranquil as a mountain lake, opaque and mysterious as the deepest ocean trench, or turbulent and merciless as the storm-whipped sea. This mutability and volatility align the element with emotions, which constantly change and flow. Water is the element of tears, of grief and sorrow. From bath water to baptism, water is cleansing and healing. Water teaches us about fluidity. It takes on the shape of any container it's in, but it also escapes from the tiniest crack. Water changes form: liquid, vapor, solid ice. From mountain springs to raging rivers, to storm drains, water always eventually finds its way back to its source: the sea. All water on earth is connected by the water cycle, so water is the element of connection and relationships. Through its link to the moon and the tides, water is the element of intuition, divination, magic, and cycles. Water is also the deepest ocean trenches of the subconscious and unconscious, full of things submerged, forgotten, and unknown.

The Interstitial Elements

Earth-Air: Ingenuity
PAGE OF SWORDS, KING OF PENTACLES

Earth-Air is the element of meditation and grounding, combining earth's stability and air's mental acuity. It's the element of clearing out and taking stock: hanging the herbs to dry, organizing the pantry, airing out the house after spring cleaning, watching dust sparkling in a sunbeam through an open window. Earth-Air is holy standing rocks, shaped by human ingenuity or by millennia of wind. It's the music of whistling rocks, woodwinds, windchimes. Earth-Air is pollinators buzzing from bloom to bloom, the yellow-green pollen hue of air in springtime, the breeze dispersing flying seeds and dandelion fluff. It's particulate matter in the air: pollution, wildfire smoke, incense smoke, perfume. It's the act of respiration, molecules of oxygen entering the body through the lungs. It's plants cleaning the air. If air is thoughts and earth the material world, Earth-Air is the element of ideas becoming reality. This is also the element of applying human intelligence to the earth's organisms and resources, for better or worse: crop rotation, renewable energies, genetic engineering, biotechnology.

Air-Fire: Belief
KING OF WANDS, KNIGHT OF SWORDS

Air-Fire is the element of revelation and epiphany. This is the crack of heat lightning flashing across the sky, the ominous rumble of danger approaching, the cataclysmic flash that illuminates a vision that can never be unseen. This is the Tower's conflagration that razes dynasties and paradigms to the ground, that tears a fiery portal in the fabric of reality, initiating new worlds. If fire is the divine spark and air is speech, Air-Fire is the Word of God. This is the element of holy belief, of prophets, saints, martyrs, and zealots. It's also the element of mystics, visionaries, and all those who dare to conceive of other realities than this. Air-Fire is the element of activists, of fiery speeches that rouse the masses to action, of civil disobedience and scathing polemics. Air-Fire is also the flashpoint when a rational debate becomes a screaming fight, when a peaceful protest becomes a riot. This is smokeless fire burning on nothing but air. This is ball lightning and will-o'-the-wisps, jet fuel and bullets. The combined power of air and fire can change the world or destroy it.

Fire-Water: Ecstasy
KNIGHT OF CUPS, QUEEN OF WANDS

Fire-Water is the element of intoxication. Literally, *firewater* is a term for strong alcohol that comes from the Ojibwe word for *fire* and *liquid*.[41] This element is the burning warmth of a whisky shot, the pain that brings pleasure, the sweaty friction of the dance floor, the moment when you give over to abandon. Fire-Water is any experience that intoxicates: the heady infatuation of new romance, the magnetic intensity of obsession, the liquid-limbed ecstasy of afterglow. This, after all, is when passionate feeling (fire) and emotional connection (water) meet. Fire-Water is the liquids of passion: spit, sweat, lubrication, ejaculation. It's bathhouses, saunas, hot springs, geysers. This elemental combination is expressed elsewhere in the tarot as Temperance, which synthesizes supposed opposites into a fluid alchemy. Fire-Water is magic. It is a quintessentially trans element, as it bridges a polarity previously thought impossible, proving the immutability of forms a lie. Both are cleansing elements: Fire purifies; water cleans. Both are also consecrating and initiating elements: trial by fire, baptism by water. This makes the Fire-Water powerful for spiritual and emotional clearing, consecrating, and initiation of all sorts, but especially for rites of passage that involve transformation.

---

41 *Merriam-Webster*, s.v. "firewater," accessed October 31, 2023, *merriam-webster.com*.

Water-Earth: Nourishment
QUEEN OF PENTACLES, PAGE OF CUPS

Water-Earth is the suck and crash of the moving shoreline, the river cutting vivid canyons over eons, the sap rising with the full moon, the tidepools teeming with strange life. Water-Earth is water plants, seaweed, and amphibious creatures that can cross the barrier of two worlds and thrive in each. This is the silty floodwaters of the Nile that render the river valley lush and fertile, the smell of wet earth after the rain, the stone skipping over the water's surface. The earth cradles water in its embrace: the sea floor, the riverbed, the water table, the silty cups of lakes. Water-Earth is the well that provides water to the village. It is blood, milk, sap—the liquids of life. It is also the water held in plants: cactus, coconut, aloe. It is juice, tinctures, oils, medicinal potions and pastes made for healing, beauty, or pleasure. Water-Earth is deeply healing and nourishing. In the form of salt water, Water-Earth was the original parent, providing the precise conditions for the first living organisms to emerge and evolve. But Water-Earth is also decomposition, rot, dead organic matter gradually liquifying as it returns to nourish the earth. This is the element of birth and death, the beginning and the end. This element can also be cloying and slippery: the mud that sucks shoes and traps vehicles, the quicksand trap awaiting the unsuspecting, the mudslide that slips whole houses and hillsides to oblivion.

Earth-Fire: Creation
PAGE OF WANDS, KNIGHT OF PENTACLES

Earth-Fire is the volcano: slow currents of magma churning beneath the ground, tunnels of fire smoldering. As the forest fire, Earth-Fire is quick and all-consuming. Its potential is cataclysmic and destructive, devouring ancient trees and entire towns into soot and ash. However, the volcano and the forest fire are also nourishing. Magma creates new, mineral-rich earth, and volcanic soil is some of the most fertile on Earth. Forest fire clears choking underbrush, releases certain types of seeds and pine cones, and in the long term nourishes the soil and keeps the forest healthy. Earth-Fire is controlled burns practiced by Indigenous peoples to caretake the land. Earth-Fire is also the oven baking bread to feed the family, the kiln firing pottery for utilitarian as well as artistic purposes, and the forge where the blacksmith shapes fire-softened metal into tools and weapons. Earth-Fire is where grounded practicality meets inspired creativity and hard work meets passionate purpose. This is the element of craftsmanship and material creation itself. This is the spark of life inside the golem, the creative spirit enfleshed. Like the flow of magma and wall of forest fire, Earth-Fire is a nearly unstoppable force. This element is excellent for initiating meaningful action in the material plane and persistent work on the things most important to us.

Air-Water: Wisdom

KING OF CUPS, QUEEN OF SWORDS

Air-Water is vapor, mist, fog, and storm. This is the element of daydreaming, of divining shapes in clouds. If air is perception and water is intuition, Air-Water can take the form of a scrying mirror. A scrying mirror is any reflective surface, including pools or bowls of water, used for achieving altered states of perception wherein visions can arise. While Air-Water can be the element of piercing the veil, it can also drop the veil over our eyes as the fog of illusion, confusion, or delusion. Air-Water is the storm dropping sheets of wind-whipped rain, the freezing heights of atmosphere that tumble raindrops into hail, the hurricane storm-surge. This face of Air-Water speaks to what can happen when thoughts and emotions clash, or when the mind and the heart conspire to inflict emotional pain and self-punishing thought spirals. By the same token, Air-Water can provide the bridge to clarify and soothe these same troubles. Air-Water is the air's kiss of dew after a dark night of the soul and the benefic rainbow after the storm. Air-Water is the element of therapy, of talking through emotions, of mindfulness practice and emotional intelligence. Air-Water is the element of mental-emotional integration and harmony, when the thinking mind and feeling heart come together to create wisdom.

Queer Applications

Working with the court cards through this elemental lens opens new, queer avenues for interpretation outside the static molds of Page/Knight/Queen/King. It liberates the cards from binary gender norms, frees them from stale hierarchy, and returns them to the living world. The court cards are not mere significator cards, not fingers pointing at your mom or your boss or a tall dark stranger. They are more than roles or functions that we can fill when called for, more than bits and pieces of our fractured psyches. The court cards are both these things and neither, a multitudinous and contradictory third, fourth, fifth, sixth thing.

The practical applications of reading the court cards as elements are numerous. When we know the elemental energies of the court cards, another layer of interpretation appears in readings. A water-heavy spread may reveal itself to be even more watery with the presence of multiple Queens. New links may reveal themselves between cards of the same element across suits. The court cards may be used in magical workings to call upon their queer energies or to represent the cardinal directions (North, South, East, West) and intercardinal directions (NE, SE, SW, NW). The court cards can also become allies in difficult times. If we feel like we're drowning, we may turn to the double-water Queen of Cups for guidance in learning to swim, or alternatively we may call upon the King of Cups or Queen of Swords (Air-Water) for an inflatable life vest to help us float above the waves.

Reading court cards as queer elements invites creative renamings and expanded interpretations. Table 2 illustrates an experiment I did while writing this essay. I took the keyword I chose for each interstitial element and paired it with the keyword for each respective suit to see what would happen. Much to my delight, this resulted in simple, effective, and surprisingly illuminating card descriptions. For example, my keyword for Air-Water is *wisdom*, for Swords is *intellect*, and for Cups is *emotion*, so the Queen of Swords becomes "Intellectual Wisdom," and the King of Cups becomes "Emotional Wisdom." This might then lead us to contemplate the similarities and differences between Intellectual Wisdom and Emotional Wisdom and how those might be manifested uniquely through the cards. Experimenting with other keywords will only lead to more insights. If I named Fire-Water *transformation* instead of *ecstasy*, for example, we would derive "Energetic Transformation" and "Emotional Transformation" for the Queen of Wands and Knight of Cups, respectively. Indeed, these descriptions feel as accurate as they do unexpected, revealing layers of interpretation and application for the cards.

	Pentacles (Earth)	Wands (Fire)	Cups (Water)	Swords (Air)
Page (Earth)	Matter	Energetic Creation	Emotional Nourishment	Intellectual Ingenuity
Knight (Fire)	Material Creation	Energy	Emotional Ecstasy	Intellectual Belief
Queen (Water)	Material Nourishment	Energetic Ectasy	Emotion	Intellectual Wisdom
King (Air)	Material Ingenuity	Energetic Belief	Emotional Wisdom	Intellect

Table 2: Card Descriptions Derived from Interstitial Elements

A Very Queer Conclusion

Now that you've read all the way to the end, I must make a confession: On one level, the words and descriptions I have laid out here are yet another attempt to categorize the uncategorizable. These are just more boxes, albeit better and more expansive ones, to slot our limited understanding into. On another level, the tarot is entirely made up—it was not handed down by a god (sorry, Hermes Trismegistus) but made by human minds and hands—so the tarot is whatever we want it to be. What, then, is the point? you ask.

Harrington puts it well: "The categorizations that humans develop are methods for our limited minds to understand and discuss that which our spirit inherently understands is possible."[42] In other words, we have to start somewhere, but we also can't stop at our limited categories and tidy conclusions.

This is precisely what tarot does best. Tarot works because it offers alternative ways of knowing ourselves and the world. When we lay out a spread, we briefly step outside ourselves to peer into our lives from other perspectives, slantwise, from the margins. Maybe that's what the court cards—these most challenging and puzzling cards—are meant to do. Challenge us. Puzzle us. One has to admit they are particularly skilled at this, always befuddling the masses and slipping between forms. Even the Golden Dawn seems to have been confused about what the court cards properly meant. In their system as outlined in *Book T* (c. 1888), the order is shuffled and the names changed, which continues to cause contention and confusion as to which is the "right" order and "right" element correspondence to this day.[43] Now, in the 21st century, we are the beneficiaries of dozens if not hundreds of tarot decks that rename the court cards, change their order, and illustrate them in new, queer, inclusive, and creative ways.

Maybe this is how the court cards like it. To always push the boundaries of our understanding. To never be rendered completely legible. To take on new forms and queer combinations every time we think we have them figured out. If we let them, the court cards can help us dissolve

---

[42] Harrington, 312.
[43] T. Susan Chang, *Tarot Correspondences: Ancient Secrets for Everyday Readers* (Llewellyn, 2018), 138.

false binaries, normative boxes, and reductive categories—both theirs and our own. So let us heed the court cards' invitation to the muddy fringes and misty margins, where we may find ourselves and each other on the edges of the known.

Let us slip into their earth bodies, water bodies, mirror bodies, molten bodies, and they into ours.

Let us listen as they teach us what it means to be transitional, what it means to transform.

TRICK MIRROR TAROT

Seventy-Eight Multifaceted Self-Reflections

By Siri Vincent Plouff

The first time I pulled a tarot card for myself in my new apartment, it was the Eight of Swords reversed. I had just broken up with my first live-in partner and had to move out within a week of finals for my first semester of graduate school. It was a difficult time, to say the least, one when my entire world upended itself. I smiled down at the card—somewhere between a smile and a smirk—and I thought to myself "of course." The Eight of Swords and the Moon cards had been haunting me constantly. I had been unsettled, unmoored, anxious without understanding why, unwilling to look deeper at what my intuition was telling me. The Moon card was trying to get me to listen to my gut, but I wasn't ready, as signified by the Eight of Swords. I was unhappy, but I hadn't yet realized that I could leave at any time. When that Eight of Swords reversed came up, it was a note of resolution: I had gotten out of the other end of the cycle.

Tarot reflects our lives because it's made and remade in new contexts, our contexts. Seventy-eight cards, each showing a different aspect of modern life. It's an old form of divination, but one that has grown from a courtly card game in the 1400s to a helpful tool for modern life. Tarot has adapted to work with us in our personal lives.

It has evolved because we have continued to make new decks offering new perspectives on the cards. There are so many decks now that can reflect different aspects of our lives. There are more decks than ever that reflect the lives of BIPOC and queer folks, for example. Tarot is used at corporate retreats as well as in the smoky rooms of occult shops.

The reason is that there's truth that we find in the cards. The tarot is a seventy-eight-sided mirror ball, reflecting the truth of our deepest selves back to us. Reading reversals turns each facet of that mirror into a trick mirror. Each reversal pulls us into a stranger world, one where you need to gather your wits about you and confront your shadow. But you know what they say: Sometimes truth is stranger than fiction, and the trick mirror of reversals doesn't disappoint.

In this essay I will lift back the curtain on why I am so passionate about reading reversals in tarot and give you some ways to begin reading them yourself. This essay belongs in an anthology about queer tarot topics because reversals themselves offer some really critical things for queer readers specifically. *The reversal acts as a subversion of the upright meanings—which creates space for interpretations that fall outside the realm of "normal society," aka heteronormative society.* The liberating aspect of reading with reversals is that each reader can come up with their own internal methodology for reading reversals.

I'm going to talk a lot about systems in this essay and ways that people can develop systems in relationship to the cards. I'm not going to tell you how you should read reversals; instead, I'm going to welcome you into the fun house where you can experiment. Reading with reversals reminds me that tarot is a deeply personal thing, that we all create our own systems. Reversals have worked their way into my own life in very intimate ways, showing up as right and necessary in my own tarot practice.

One of the reasons we show up as queer tarot readers is to find ourselves in the cards. There are certain complex layers that we might need to undo—getting beyond the heteronormativity of the overculture, finding yourself, moving in new spaces. Opening up the layers of queerness within also brings us deeply in touch with our desires.

Desire can be frightening. There is a reason that Venus is tied to the Morning Star is tied to Lucifer is tied to Babalon. Desire devours. Queer desire has been shunned and othered, shut out of "regular" society. Queer desire is its own reversal, a subversion of what we think is normal. Queerness presents a different model of desire than we have been told to believe is "normal." When we look back at some of the most "traditional" first decks that people choose most often, we don't see queer protagonists in the cards. In so many cases, the figures on the cards don't even reflect our reality: There are no people of color, no visibly queer people, no disabled people, no fat people in the *Rider Waite Smith* deck, nor the *Thoth*, nor the *Marseilles*.

We have to make the conscious decision to see ourselves in these decks. We have to tilt the mirror the tarot is showing us, look back from behind the looking glass to make sense of ourselves.

Buying Your Ticket to the Fun House: Reasons to Read or Not Read with Reversals

Reversals are still a curiously dividing topic among tarot readers. When I bought my first deck back in . . . 2006? . . . the little white book that came with the deck included meanings for reversals. When I bought my second deck in 2008, it came with a whole book on tarot, 200+ pages of information that I couldn't get enough of. In those 200+ pages, there was a detailed description of each card's reversed meaning, and I took that seriously. Surely, if the creator of the deck spent so much time on reversals, they were an important facet of the meaning of the tarot, and

I *had* to read with them. I took reversals for granted as I was learning tarot and never looked back.

But not every tarot reader uses reversals. In fact, most of my friends who are professional cartomancers *don't* read with them. That is not to say that they are not excellent readers. They are the readers I go to when I don't trust myself to give an unbiased reading in the privacy of my own home, in the comfort of my assumptions. When these readers work with tarot, it is not that the reversed meanings of each card aren't present; it's much more about the placement of the cards. The World card in a position of "what you stand to lose" is, after all, devastating. So, of course, it is still possible to get the myriad meanings out of a single card.

There aren't as many resources on learning to read tarot reversals for this reason. So many readers don't deem them necessary, and there are so many other facets to the deck that you can learn first. Doing a quick Google search in the writing of this essay, I was only able to find two or three books that are specifically about tarot reversals. They are both great resources. *The Complete Book of Tarot Reversals* by Mary K. Greer is a must-read for anyone interested in this topic.[44] She goes in depth into each and every one of the cards. *Tarot Reversals for Beginners* by Leeza Robertson is also a fantastic resource.[45] She even goes into the ramifications of reversals and their energy in terms of spellwork, which is a fascinating area of study and practice. There are a few other books, but I have not read them and cannot speak to them. The thing is, reversals open up whole new avenues of reading, and each one looks different to each reader.

When a card comes up reversed, it is not simply the opposite of what it means when it comes out upright. Sometimes the reversed cards are more like slipping sideways into a weird, unintended consequence of the upright position. In your own personal readings

---

44   Mary K. Greer, *The Complete Book of Tarot Reversals* (Llewellyn Publications, 2002).
45   Leeza Robertson, *Tarot Reversals for Beginners: Five Approaches to Reading Upside-Down Cards* (Llewellyn Publications, 2018).

with yourself, you might find that the relationship you have with your deck determines the meaning of the reversed cards. It's an intimacy that isn't written into the little white book that came with your deck.

The easier way to read tarot is, of course, to simplify it. Smooth over those difficult edges, learn the upright meanings, and stick with them. Pesky cards that turn out the wrong direction shouldn't be your problem to deal with, right? But here's the thing: We all have bent edges. Especially if you are queer, you might need to find yourself reflected in these Other meanings. Perhaps you're kinky, and the Lovers card in the *Rider-Waite-Smith* deck, a heterosexual couple with an angel presiding over them, doesn't entice you as much as the reversed image we see in the Devil card. In this card, a man and a woman are in chains, being presided over by a Devil who looks somehow upset with you—ready to punish and titillate.

Reversals are a subversion. They are a fascinating way of reading the cards and bring so much added nuance to the deck. It makes sense to me to see the reversed cards as not just the opposite of the upright cards, but as windows into a world where everything is not as it seems. For those of us who already live on the margins, we are accustomed to getting curious about what isn't said openly.

There are not very many resources about learning to read tarot this way. I have spent the last thousand words or so convincing you to read with reversals, so now I feel it is my duty to help you find some ways into this style of reading.

The Green Room: Getting Comfortable with Reversals

When you first get started reading reversals, it may take a while for you to get comfortable with seeing the cards overturned. That's why I want to suggest some ways to get comfortable with them, to greet them, and to become casual acquaintances.

A lot of people ask if you can ask the tarot yes/no questions. There are good spreads for reading yes/no questions out there, but another way of reading yes/no questions is to divide the deck in two, reverse one half of the deck, and shuffle well. Then, ask your yes/no question. If the card comes out upright, it's a yes. If it comes out reversed, it's a no.

Reversals are also a way of gauging the energy of your deck. For example, when I go to an event and read for a lot of people, I will shuffle the deck messily at the beginning of the event in order to get some reversed cards. When I put cards back in the deck, I am not concerned about whether they are reversed or not. Then, after all of the readings have been done, I go through the deck and gently turn every card the same direction. This is a way of "clearing" the deck of the energy from that event. In her brilliant book on reversals, Mary K. Greer recommends that you turn all cards to face the same way after *every* reading as a way of clearing the deck. Personally, this practice feels like too much to me, but you can choose your own energetic container. If you are a professional reader and need space between clients, by all means, right the cards after every client.

There are also some incredible decks that play around with the concepts of reversals. *The Tarot of Oppositions* is a deck from Lo Scarabeo that shows the upright meaning on the "top" of the card, but then the image transforms into the reversed meaning for that card.[46] Depending on which side is upright when you pull the card, you can very easily see the difference between the reversed and upright meanings. I own this deck and was playing around with it during the writing of this essay, and I think it is a fantastic deck if you are interested in getting comfortable with the basic meanings of the cards. I will say that it does tend to lean

---

46   Michelle D'Aloisio and Pierluca Zizzi, *Tarot of Oppositions* (Lo Scarabeo, 2021).

into "reversals as the opposite meaning" a little too much for my taste, but it is a fantastic concept and is so helpful for someone learning tarot.

Another deck that plays around with the concept of reversals is the *Corrupted Tarot* by Wyrmwood Gaming.[47] This is a gorgeous anthology deck with many different artists coming together. The concept of the deck is that the reversed meaning is the primary meaning for the card, "corrupting" the deck. I've also been playing around with this deck while writing this essay. Wyrmwood is a tabletop role-playing game accessory company, so this deck is definitely influenced by *Dungeons & Dragons* aesthetically, but the artwork is not the stereotypical artwork that you might immediately think of. The interpretations of the cards feel closer to the trick mirror effect that I look for in reversals.

I'm sure there are plenty of other decks that play around with tarot meanings in similar ways, but you definitely don't need a special deck to learn how to read tarot reversals. I include these decks because it can be enjoyable for the deck collectors out there to add to your existing collection.

Sleight of Hand: Shuffling to Get Reversals

Generally speaking, I don't care how you shuffle. It's a question that comes up fairly often in tarot classes, and it surprises me each time. That being said, there is a bit of an art to shuffling in order to obtain reversals, and it depends a little bit on your perspective.

My favorite method for years was to simply drop the deck onto the table I was using to read, move the cards around with my hands like churning waves, and then pull them all back together into some semblance of shape. Then I would shuffle traditionally and draw the cards for my reading. This is a perfectly fine and acceptable way of shuffling! Shuffling this way can also get you down and dirty with the

---

47   Wyrmwood, *The Corrupted Tarot* (Wyrmwood Gaming, 2022).

cards, breaking them out of their glass case. It brings the cards down to earth.

My own way of shuffling now is a little bit more deliberate. I shuffle the deck once or twice, then divide it into three piles. I reverse one of those piles. Then I shuffle the deck for as long as it would take to incorporate those three piles back into one another. This way there is a good chance that you will have at least one reversed card in your reading, but it will also perhaps alarm you if you get all reversed cards. That would signify that there are significant issues and that you need to take extra caution with the reading in this case.

Exhibition Hall: Different Ways to Read Reversals

Throughout *The Complete Book of Tarot Reversals,* Mary K. Greer describes in depth twelve different ways to read with reversals. I actually didn't read this book until fairly recently—2021—and it gave me a lot to think about in terms of the different styles that people use to read these cards. I'm not going to go in depth on all of these, but I did want to outline them here so that you can start thinking about what makes the most sense to you:

12. Blocked or Resisted: The energy normally described by the card is blocked. This is a very common way of seeing reversals.

11. Projected: You may be projecting something onto others that you actually need to deal with yourself.

10. Delayed, Difficult, or Unattainable: If you are working toward a goal, you may be delayed in getting to it.

9. Inner, Unconscious, Private: The energy is intended only for the querent, and/or it is an unconscious energy and the querent may not even be aware of it. It's an area to journal about to get more clear about your needs.

8. New or Dark Moon: This is a tradition of reversals that comes out of working with round decks. Essentially, when the card is fully reversed, it represents the New Moon Phase (beginnings, unconscious, hidden). As the round card turns, the angle of the card indicates the moon phase.

7. Overturning or Changing Direction: This means realizing that something isn't working and trying to break out of the cycle.

6. "No" or "Not" the Upright Meaning: This is particularly helpful for readings when you are trying to make decisions.

5. Over- or Undercompensating: This pushes the card's meaning to a more extreme place, being unable to see clearly because you are over- or underinvested in this aspect of the reading.

4. Misused or Misdirected: This means a faulty start, misdirection, or bad timing.

3. "Re" words: Review, Retry, Reconsider: There is something about the original assessment that is not working, so you need to review it.

2. Rectification: This is the heart of the problem, and you need to heal it by "turning the energy upright."

1. Unconventional Interpretation: This card needs to be interpreted differently than you would interpret the card in its upright form.[48]

I definitely wouldn't advise utilizing all of these methods right off the bat. There are some methods that I use all the time, and others that simply do not work for me. The best way to figure out what ways reversals work for you is through experimentation. Look at this list and narrow down the approaches that make the most sense to you. Then, for an extended period of time (could be a week of

---

48   Greer, *The Complete Book of Tarot Reversals*.

daily draws, could be a full month of readings), read reversals with that method. Figure out what resonates. Write everything down in your journal.

Spending Time in the Fun House

Entering a fun house at the circus is like stepping into another world. It is a space where you can't necessarily trust your senses, a place where things are distorted. The fun house is a place of experimentation for the circus architects. Perhaps you would like to think of this part of learning as finding your own fun house within the deck.

The one thing that I will ask you to do is to put ideas of "accuracy" out of your mind. Folding in the kind of intuitive connection I'm encouraging in your tarot practice requires looking at things through squinted eyes. Learning to read this way means that you get a break from worrying about how things "should" be and instead focus on your own personal meanings.

Reading reversals requires time, and over time your intuition will take over when the card comes up inverted. It's also important to note that while I was learning tarot, I only ever used one deck at a time. Using the same deck over and over and over, day in and day out, for every reading large or small that you do for yourself, means that you get to know that deck particularly well. If this is your first time exploring the weird, queer, slant meanings of reversals, you may want to choose one deck to use consistently for this purpose. It will be an exercise in intimacy, getting to know just one deck over the course of time. I do think that it would be helpful to choose a deck that has reversed meanings for the cards in its little book. Even if all you have is a few keywords, that will help you by being a jumping-off point.

When I learned reversals, I didn't force it. I took for granted that they were an essential part of tarot, so I dutifully read the reversal information in the books that came with my decks and applied it to all of my readings.

There are a couple of allies you will take with you on this journey. Like I said earlier, I recommend using just one deck to get started. Get to know both your relationship with that deck as well as your relationship to the upside-down cards. The other ally is a notebook.

Exercise: Experimentation Chamber

One of my favorite ways of learning a new tarot deck—or in this case, developing your own meaning system—is to create a notebook for a full study of the deck. Now, this is a lot of work. I was not this methodical as I was learning tarot. Here's a way of looking at it: Set aside a specific amount of time regularly to work on this project. It doesn't need to be an hour every day, but it does need to be regular. That will help you to keep the momentum in developing your own system of reversals.

- ❖ Take a notebook that is at least seventy-eight pages long and write out the name of one tarot card on the top of each page. Yes, you will need a full page for this. The top third of the page is going to be a reference for your personal associations with that particular card.

- ❖ Draw a line. Below that line, start with all of your assumed meanings for what that card reversed might mean.

- ❖ Now shuffle your cards. Pull a card and write out your basic ideas about that card in the first third.

- ❖ Flip the card upside down, and set a timer for a minute. Stare at the card; immerse yourself in its energy.

- ❖ Freewrite in your tarot journal about all of the things that came up for you as you were staring at the reversed version of the card. What did the card say to you? What did it whisper? What did it shout? Write out *everything*—even if it's contradictory. Chances are, the different and sometimes contradictory meanings that come up in this exercise are going to be applied in different readings.

If you're reading this and feeling like it's a bit too much for you at the moment, there are other ways of learning the reversed meanings. You could learn it the way I did—slow and steady, allowing there to be reversed cards in your readings and figuring out what each card means as you go.

This is also a good place to collect daily readings while experimenting with what style of reversal you want to explore. Choose a section of your notebook to explore a particular style of reading with reversals, and see what resonates the most with you.

Begin to purposefully incorporate reversed meanings into your daily tarot draw. This essentially requires pulling one card and reading it twice. First, pull a card to represent how your day is going to go. Just a regular old daily draw. Interpret the meaning of the card in its upright position. Then, take some time to read the card in its reversed position. Think about what this card would mean for your day if it came up reversed and expand on that. For added analysis, look back on your interpretations at the end of the day and see what made the most sense.

Above all, the thing that will allow you to enjoy working with reversals is enjoying the process. Learning tarot in any form is learning a new language, and in order to learn a new language, you have to practice that language. That means doing a *ton* of readings. Whether that's a daily card pull or a weekly mind/body/soul reading, or practicing with your roommates, friends, family, and loved ones.

While you're doing this, I strongly encourage you to go deep and use one deck for a specific period of time. Reversals are tricky beasts that change and shift based on the decks we're using. This is why I so strongly recommend learning reversals one deck at a time, if you have multiple decks. One way that I have found to be a really beautiful relationship-building exercise with decks is to use one deck over the course of one lunar cycle.

Mirrorball Tarot

When you come out the other side of this level of depth and study with your deck, you can feel like you are the hero returning from the Underworld Journey. You are Inanna, returning to the light. You are Persephone, balancing death and life. As a queer reader, you are also now able to bring your own subversions to life in your readings. You may feel that the deck has been a friend, gently (or perhaps not-so-gently) bringing yourself into a deeper understanding of yourself.

This is when the metaphor of the trick mirror transforms into the mirror ball. There are infinite facets reflecting back on us, allowing us to truly see what is happening from many different angles.

You could say that the tarot spokesperson for reversals is the Hanged One. Often depicted upside down, the Hanged One represents many things. They represent a moment of stillness, of waiting for the other shoe to drop. The Hanged One knows that there is more information out there, that perhaps it's too soon to make a decision. They encourage us to wait for more information; they let us know that we aren't seeing things as clearly as we would like to.

Reversed, the Hanged One appears in a reading right-side-up. Here they are rising above their shackles, instead of hanging by them. It's almost as if the Hanged One energy is only uncrossed when we have taken the time to examine all perspectives.

For me, the Hanged One shows up in several personal ways. The first deity that I really began a relationship with was Odin, the Hanged God. Whenever the Hanged One shows up, it feels like a wink from him. Odin's primary lessons for me have to do with learning, wisdom, and the wisdom to figure out when I'm on the wrong (or right) track.

Of course, I learned reversals concurrently with upright meanings; there was no other way.

When I really began studying the tarot, I was at a crossroads. I was living with my boyfriend, unhappy because I felt like I constantly had to prove that my femme bisexuality was valid. I felt trapped by the assumption of heterosexuality and terrified of exploring my queerness because that would mean turning my world upside down.

I wanted to subvert expectations, to revel in my femininity, to be happy with the person I was currently seeing, but all of the messages that I was getting from other queer people that I knew and different media told me that I needed to have at least been with women or nonbinary people before settling down with a man. This was, of course, something that I rebelled against in my mind, so I doubled down. Instead of seeing the ways in which I truly wasn't happy in that relationship, I felt like I needed to hang on to it to prove something to myself. It wasn't something true, but it was something that felt true to me at the time.

Tarot has brought me back to myself over and over again. Being queer for me has been so much about self-discovery and learning to be comfortable with myself. The Eight of Swords Reversed was a wake-up call for me. A big part of the reason I left the relationship I was in was so that I could explore more of my queer identity. I was pulled into the miraculous, glittering mirrorball life that I have now. As an out bisexual nonbinary person, so much of my life has been looking at things from new angles and finding nuance. Reversals have helped me to do that. Being queer will keep you on your toes—so we enter the fun house, over and over. Reversed tarot cards are the trick mirrors that show us all of our edges, even and especially the scary ones. But that's the thrill of life, isn't it?

There's a sense of humor to tarot that can't really be explained or replicated. Laughter, like an audience taking in the circus show. Are you the one laughing, or are the cards? Which of us is truly on display? While I was working on this essay, I hit a stumbling block. I decided to pull a card for myself to figure out if I was even going somewhere good with it. I got the Eight of Swords—reversed, of course. I smiled to myself, and I knew that my intuition was leading me down the right path.

A TREATISE ON QUEERING SYMBOLS

By Taylor Ursula

threads of queerness, like the threads of tarot, weave together within us in layers, tendrils of meaning forged through time and experience. no single moment nor single image nor card within the deck can define the complexity of the narrative we live and breathe and discover. rather, the tapestry must come together through the fullness of contextualization and recontextualization, a process we embark upon as long as we are engaged in the practice of personal and social evolution. this evolution has manifested within many of us as an act of *queering*, in which we become conscious to the influences that have shaped us and begin to question their hold on our identities as individuals and as communities.

I

queering symbols has always been a practice for those of us who have had to create a world that better reflects our experiences and that actually holds space for us. for as long as symbols have been used to create meaning on a collective scale, symbols have been deconstructed and modified to better identify the marginalized within that collective scale. symbols that are oppressive, exclusive, or limited in their scope become shapeshifted into those that are more accepting or representative in the hands of those for whom they deny or omit.

similarly, we have historically queered language in such a way that it becomes part of our arsenal rather than our allowing it to remain weaponized against us by those who reject or deny us. this process serves as an act of reclaiming the right to fit into our world. this act serves not only to make our own existence tolerable, but to communicate to others around us that their theoretical existence could serve as a beacon for community and camaraderie, an anchor point for trust to grow in living out these identities and seeing possibilities of future acceptance on the collective horizon.

we queer symbols and language to pry them free from the normative narrative, to detach them from the binds of the binary, to bend and reshape them into something that can more closely define us as individuals as well as members within the communities we forge and share. we queer symbols to step out of and shed the lingering weight and harm caused by stories that have been manipulated to outcast us from worlds we were designed to be a part of. we queer symbols to repair the harm of being born into such worlds and to find ways to reconnect with the greater ecosystem. "by changing our collective behavior," Alice Sparkly Kat writes in the introduction of their book *Postcolonial Astrology*, "we are able to change what we see in the stars by changing ourselves."[49]

in the same way, we have historically queered the body, stripping it of the projected expectations and values of heteronormativity and traditional identities in such a way that grants us the freedom to take on a physical presentation that better "defines" the person living within the vessel. we engage in a simultaneous mission of separating from the parts of ourselves that seem to betray us and adopting shapes and forms that speak to the otherness that we contain. this continuous act of rupture and repair, while vulnerable, deepens our ability to trust ourselves, our environment, and the relationship that grows between them. it instills

---

49 Alice Sparkly Kat, *Postcolonial Astrology* (North Atlantic Books, 2021), 5.

in us the knowledge that no matter how much we continue to evolve and change, we are collaborating with a broader whole that holds and witnesses and accepts us, even while the systems we live within continue to reject us. this journey, while daunting, affords us the opportunity to connect with a quality of life that is otherwise gatekept by those who wish to maintain the status quo.

for me, queering the body began in my teens and unfolded well into my thirties. as a result of a constant sense of otherness generated by a youth spent in predominantly white spaces, I created a practice of isolating parts of my body that I felt betrayed my assigned gender—pronounced biceps, broad shoulders. I wrestled with parts of my body that did not fit into mainstream standards of beauty—my wide nose, breasts living fully separate lives. the parts of me that seemed to please my peers became a source of hyperfocus before becoming completely alien to me. I found that changing those "undesirable" parts through piercings and tattoos allowed me to somehow accept myself. it was empowering to change what I could not reconcile, a rite of passage and a tool of reframing my experience in my own skin. using ink and metal to create new stories on canvas that had otherwise been designated as *other* and allowing for intentional and deliberate demarcations to overwrite painful stories buried beneath the skin gave me new life. it became a means of identifying others like me, others moving through their own journeys of reframing and reclaiming, and through this identification, we began supporting and celebrating each other in doing the same, forging community around our ability to continually shapeshift as the collective narrative targets and pressures us to conform.

I appreciate being in a place where I can now look back and reflect on the layers I've accumulated thus far. I have so much admiration for the clumsy steps I took in finding meaning along the way and hold as much reverence for the confusion I felt in my nonstop Celtic cross phase as I do for my clunky, soft stud phase. it is comforting to witness the layers continuously contextualize and recontextualize as they gel, witnessing the evolution of the meaning as it takes flexible shape. until the next layer is discovered and adhered. this process is ever facilitated by the evolution of the symbology and language made available to me, and in this relationship, we see how queering is an ongoing process occurring not just within the person but between the person and their environment—as above, so below, as within, so without. what changes outside of me allows me to change what I see within myself, which then changes how I see what exists outside of me, and so on.

I saw this process extend and blend into my relationship with astrology first. I was fortunate enough to begin my focused astrological studies at a time when I was within increasingly queer spaces with people who were finding a similar pathway. by operating within queer community learning spaces, I participated in conversations that pried open the dialogue of the binary, dismantling my traditionally gendered assumptions and seeing the results trickle outward into my delineations, recognizing when the highly gender-defined narratives as taught to me by astrological authorities like Robert Hand could not possibly be applied as such to the people I was connecting with through this knowledge. collaboratively, we were learning how to separate the human from the heteronormative.

tracing back these translations to the traditional framework of Hellenistic astrology, I came to understand that the origins of this astrology framework emerged with the establishment of the Roman Empire, during which Greek astronomers were called to bring an end to the matriarchal power of Virgo into Scorpio (recognize they share a similar symbol!) by dividing these femme processes of *matter* (mother) with a patriarchy-enforcing symbol Libra in order to put a stop to, or at least create boundaries around, procreation and sexuality.[50] understanding that the enforced gender roles and rules we've been coerced into adopting have been designed as an element of colonization and industrialization allows for conscientiously embodying a new understanding of

---

50   Demetra George and Douglas Bloch, *Asteroid Goddesses: The Mythology, Psychology, and Astrology of the Re-emerging Feminine* (Ibis Press, 1986, 2003), 124.

being that incorporates both the ancient and more modern worlds. we continue our experimentation with not a singular way of being but rather the both/and/other model—in a sense, keeping the parts that feel definitive and continuing to adjust for where more nuance is needed.

I found it surprising that studying hypnosis lent so deeply to this work. it is through being led through past life regression myself on many occasions, and later leading others through the process, that helped me shape a deeper perspective around the historically cruel and unjust nature of humanity. through self and other, I've been able to open up to the recognition that within us lives not only the experience of being ostracized and othered in this lifetime but in scores of lifetimes before. lifetimes wherein we lived in times somehow more oppressive, violent, and limited than the present. lifetimes wherein these harmful structures that oppress us currently were built and created and seeded. through this inner journey myself and witnessing it through others, I began to recognize patterns of the past in which *choice* was rarely possible and only afforded to those with enough status and stature to create the rules. in which *choice* was, as it has become once more, a luxury.

these revelations are both disheartening and catalyzing, providing new choices in the wake of what we have seen: to awaken the desire to live in such a way that we've been denied many times in the past. to trust the ability to see ourselves differently than the world allows us to be seen. to walk and live within the sense of self that has been cultivated from one lifetime into the next. within the pages of *Many Lives, Many Masters*, Brian L. Weiss recognizes the catharsis of healing that occurs in layers as we continue to confront these past-life memories, and the symbols contained within them, effectively setting ourselves free from their grip as we move to "release" these images and their weight in our subconscious.[51] in sharing his ongoing regression work with his client, he witnesses these milestones of freedom from deeply

---

51 Brian L. Weiss, *Many Lives, Many Masters* (Touchstone, 1988).

buried psychological symptoms as a direct result of the understanding gained in this revealing process.

exploring this process of separating from traditional images within tarot took me longer, as tarot was my oldest study, and our relationship extends back into childhood. those traditional images had long been programmed in my mind as the default for reading. with the Rider-Waite as the most prevalent and accessible deck, in part because it lives within the public domain, most of us have been raised on these homogenous images of European whiteness and heteronormativity and have had to forge a sense of identity around misshapen and ill-fitting stories we don't recognize as originating organically within us. detaching astrological symbols through conversations and revelations with others helped me begin this process of queering these symbols and ignited in me a desire to see a *less-is-more* approach within the cards, while many decks I came across continued to enforce the thin, able- and-white-bodied rhetoric of the Western world. this ultimately manifested in designing my debut deck, PORTALS,[52] which features many disembodied entities representative of an imagined whole. this allowed me to invite the reader to fill in the blanks and insert themselves or others in their sphere into the frame for more personal interpretation, stripping traditional images down into parts and creating a configuration that holds space for meaning without assigning or enforcing it. in my own way, I was separating meaning from heteronormative design and allowing new narratives to inform the interpretation. when culturally saturated symbols are eradicated, when the eye is not accosted with harmful and limiting assumptions, new intuitive processes are allowed to unfold and inform.

these intuitive processes were ultimately initiated for me through the journey of exploring hypnosis, and it was in those months of study and practice that my deck began to reveal itself to me. while past life regression allowed me to access the crux of the narratives we seek to

---

52 Taylor Ursula, *PORTALS* (So Much Potential, 2022).

escape, explorative hypnosis allowed me to begin the practice of manipulating images and entities within the subconscious space. the prehypnotic task of ascribing shapes and colors to feelings and states of being facilitates the hypnotic task of going within to then attempt to change those feelings and states of being into different shapes and brighter colors, further demonstrating the process of change within revealing subsequent changes outside of us. in discovering the neuroplasticity that grows with practice, I grew more comfortable confronting elements within the subconscious that had been as limiting and oppressive as the elements and symbols I had to endure in the world around me.

over time, this confrontation grows gentler and can even become playful when we approach these connections with curiosity, again revealing the layers in which we can modify and recontextualize our experiences as well as our relationship to that ritual of modification. each act of engagement can create a new form that is both independent of as well as carved from the previous forms. zooming out a bit, there is queerness too in the practice of focusing on *feelings* through acts of creativity and intuition rather than seeking a more "rational" approach that produces or contributes to some form of emotional dissociation. acknowledgment of the contradiction within us is known to free us, and yet this simple act is often suppressed by the structures that seek homogeneity.

deeper layers of expression become accessible to us when we subvert the singularity of biology by blending traditionally phallic and yonic symbols in such a way that emulsifies multitudes of gender across the conscious and subconscious domains. I admit that as an artist in the process of designing this deck, I was not fully aware of this decision, identifying only upon reflection the drive to create worlds and landscapes in which a both/all approach can be applied. this practice can facilitate our instinctual identification with the image as a whole in the same way that perhaps seeing the first and last letters of a word can help you fill in the remainder, with the idea being that many combinations

herein are possible and there is often no "wrong" word. this blending signals to the subconscious the permission to embody the fullness of one's energies and experiences rather than continuing to *other* them to fit the environment that seeks to sterilize and categorize them. with each viewing, we encounter the potential to conjure entirely new connotations and create new layers of meaning and experimentation.

in developing the court cards in PORTALS, it was a difficult decision to leave the court significations as is. I have intentions down the line of exploring a structure of some sort that could fairly represent the vague hierarchy that structures the evolution of how the cards move and act without using gendered language, but I felt that I was not able to comfortably do so while making this deck without taking further time to exhaustively research structures designed by others that I could potentially and unknowingly be appropriating. I felt too that queer culture already practices an open defiance and reframing of the gendered implications of *king* and *queen* and that these designated titles speak much more to roles we are all capable of playing and stepping into. the invitation stands to examine with nuance the different roles we may feel called to represent within different contexts, in our intimate relationships as well as across communities or spaces, and engage in the curiosity of the fulfillment and wholeness afforded by the recognition of the *many* within us.

two of swords: a beam of light points upward toward a crescent moon

justice: a sword and a blooming rose flanked by scales

queens: all incomplete bodies, each a different piece of the body exposed or detailed

king of pentacles: buds in various states of bloom surrounding mountain peaks

high priestess: a gown without a body

five of cups: beads of water moving through a canal into an opening of light

chariot: a triangle between mirrored moons penetrating a winding river

page of wands: a hand with fingers dipped in gold igniting a golden flame

ten of pentacles: castle towers surrounded by rosebuds piercing into a valley

the star: a crystal aflame pointing into a gridded V

the emperor: a compass exploring peaks and valleys

the empress: traditionally femme planets stacked under nature penetrating a valley

three of cups: blooming tulips closely nestled

four of wands: castle towers flanked by rosebuds surrounded by staffs of flame

king of wands: a mountaintop on fire embracing the cosmos

nine of cups: the moon dripping into stemmed goblets

II

fundamental to our alienation from our multitudes are the structures that have come to alienate us from our natural world. colonization, of course, began with the stealing of land and followed with the exploitation and destruction of its people and its resources. within this practice began the evaluation system of all of earth's beings as a means of determining rank and entitlement to the earth's collective resources. this unnatural hierarchical process divided us from our natural state at the same time that it forever altered the rhythm of our being. the closer we appeared to resemble or embody our animal counterparts, the lesser we were thought to be as creatures. we know that before industrialization we were well-versed in practices that revered and honored the land we lived on, working diligently to protect that which fed and nourished us.

we engage in this work of deprogramming as the world around us fails to heed the signs that our earth is preparing for a factory reset, and we are called to recognize where it is crucial to reject the modern traditions that compel us to devalue the earth and to reestablish ways in which we can reenter into collaborative commitments to our environment.

therefore, another layer of queerness involves extracting ourselves from our current capitalistic landscape and repositioning ourselves within the original contexts from which we initially emerged and learned and grew. we need to place meaning and importance back onto the indigenous environment and the symbolism of the before-time, consciously de-centering ourselves as the main characters of the universe and remembering that we once lived in relationship with our world before the powers that be grew hungry for domination. this act helps recalibrate us back to our primal psychological instincts, because within all of us lives the memory of precivilization and the codes and symbolism of nature we lived by.

one exploration of this lies in Jung's argument that humans "inherit" the knowledge of the collective unconscious, that we all have access to the archetypal journeys of containing the "motives and images" that we live by within our conscious choices and actions.[53] in remembering and consciously incorporating a way of existing that predates the patriarchal lens through which we currently live and recognizing that we make up many of the threads that weave into the universal tapestry but that we are not the tapestry itself. by radicalizing our perception of our *individuality*—a concept that itself is historically radical—as it is informed by our environment, and by choosing to honor and work with the environment rather than honoring false systems that have been built to somehow surpass it, we stand to deepen and strengthen our self-perception in the recognition that it is one of many layers.

in PORTALS, I attempt this process of radicalization and invite the reader into the same process, by extracting as much human content

---

[53] Brian L. Weiss, *Many Lives, Many Masters* (Touchstone, 1988), 106.

from the image as possible. this not only invites the queering of seeing ourselves step directly into any setting or scene without obstruction of identification, but by doing so also invites in the capacity to discover meaning within said scene without automatically centering our human selves within the narrative. of course, in reading the tarot, we are engaging in a highly subjective practice, as we are often seeking insight into our personal situations, be they dreams or crises. but it is possible to practice seeking guidance in such a way that allows us to again engage in recontextualizing how those dreams or crises are supported by or rooted in our broader environment. *this practice of questioning facilitates the externalization of this new context and allows us to integrate this new context into how we engage in our world and environment moving forward.*

one way we've begun to bridge this violent separation from our natural state is by covering our bodies with the animals and symbols of wildness that have been stripped from our environment, that have been deemed dangerous or otherwise incompatible with the civilized lifestyle of the so-called first world. on a social scale, we queer ourselves by culturally and socially separating from traditionally sanctioned ambitions that seek to otherwise separate us from and strip us of a sense of spirit and connectedness—not one of centrality—that turns human relationality into a hierarchy that oppresses us both collectively as well as within our internal systems. queerness then is and has been an act of creating and holding space for the otherness and multiplicity within us, which then spreads into creating and holding space for the otherness in others. exploring animalism as both the nonhuman and the noncivilized other within us, recognizing where we are different and where we are the same, and holding reverence for those intrinsic relationships.

part of deconstructing heteronormativity is deconstructing our attachment to the structures that produced and are reinforced by the nuclear family and the traditional gender model we've been conditioned to operate within. we must reconsider the broader roles we've been expected to perform within the capitalistic world, the forms of "success" we have been driven to attain, and muster the strength, courage, and humility to separate from the grandiosity that has come to define the ideal human experience. in connecting to deeper, more authentic purpose, passion, and capacity, we attune ourselves to our soul essence and natural purpose. we've internalized the inherent entitlement to our earth's resources as a means of not just *surviving* earth but somehow *besting* it. it is critical to remember at this time that the earth is resplendent with gifts as the elite prepare to colonize and further destroy the rest of space. there is a need to further decentralize culturally, to acknowledge and accept that themes of hyper-independence are extremely Western and, in particular, American and serve to deplete us of the kind of nurturance that can only be fulfilled through community and intentional connection with our environment. our own unburdening must be coupled with the unburdening of those around us, be they family or stranger. the work we do to disarm our internalized trauma, which we hopefully perform on a regular basis, is not to allow us to establish a sense of hyper-individuation, but rather to assist others in our shared realms to do the same in an effort to uplift the collective.

I remember first witnessing this phenomenon and becoming conscious of this possibility, of unlearning human centrality and refocusing on the natural landscape, in Kim Krans's iconic *Wild Unknown* deck,[54] in which the narratives of the tarot are depicted purely through natural creatures and elements. this presentation allowed me to detach the symbolism of the cards from the white cis lens so heavily enforced by the *Rider-Waite* deck and those that have been designed in its structure. (there are several other decks showcasing nonhuman forms, but these decks tend to be more novelty in fashion and focus on a singular type of animal.) we have seen other decks celebrate this exploration in various ways, such as the *Animism Tarot*,[55] the *Wildwood Tarot*,[56] the

---

54   Kim Krans, *The Wild Unknown* (Harper Collins, 2016).
55   Joanna Cheung, *The Animism Tarot* (Rainbow of Crazy, 2013).
56   Mark Ryan, John Matthews, and Will Worthington, *The Wildwood Tarot* (Welbeck Publishing, 2021).

Gentle Tarot,[57] and Charlie Claire Burgess's *Fifth Spirit Tarot*.[58] these decks anchor the reader into gender neutrality while entwining elements of nature as a means of reframing the experiences of our day-to-day lives, depicting us in direct relationship to this exploration and allowing us to engage in a reclaiming of physical and spiritual sovereignty that becomes woven into our personal framework.

chrysalis (the hanged one): a butterfly encased in its hard shell in space

two of pentacles: a budding seed and its roots stretching into the earth

the magician: Mercury and accompanying planets aligning in orbit

four of pentacles: a lemon tree's roots outstretching the bottom of its pot

ace of cups: a glowing beach at dawn

the hermit: an elusive doorway opening in the middle of the forest

five of pentacles: dried orange slices circling a pool

the fool: a theoretical aerial view of the universe

page of cups: a hummingbird skimming the surface of a lake

six of pentacles: outstretched hands grasping at an abundance of oranges

ten of swords: the sun rises in the pitch black of desert mountains

temperance: elements of nature converging in harmony

ten of cups: a rainbow spanning a starlit waterfall surrounded by blooming roses

page of pentacles: a monstera leaf slowly unfurling in the ether

strength: butterflies float gently in front of a panther's watchful eyes

knight of pentacles: a honey bee pollinating flowers

page of swords: a hawk dancing in and out of the frames of consciousness

---

57 Mariza Ryce Aparicio-Tovar, *The Gentle Tarot* (Self-Published, 2021).
58 Charlie Claire Burgess, *Fifth Spirit Tarot* (Hay House, 2022).

the tower: lava flowing around a radiating mountain

eight of pentacles: a harvest of produce surrounded by baskets

III

as outlined in the preceding lists, there are several examples with POR-TALS that showcase these themes explored within this essay. CHRYS-ALIS might be my favorite, as it is the biggest leap from its counterpart in the Rider-Waite, the Hanged Man. the idea of moving away from the concept of *hanging* was something I decided upon in conversation with fellow artist Elia Diane Fushi Bekene (aka Care), who was in the process of creating their tarot deck, *Ancestral Healing Tarot*,[59] at the same time I was finishing up PORTALS. we discussed how, as Black folx navigating a cultural narrative of normalized violence, we were not interested in any portrayal of *hanging* regardless of the context or the process. it is evident within the *Rider-Waite* deck that this image, of a haloed man hanging from his ankle mounted to a cross, suggests an inversion of the image of Jesus on the cross, and many readers draw the connection between the Hanged Man and the influences of Neptune and/or the essence of Pisces. A. E. Waite himself described the figure within the Hanged Man as a "seeming martyr" and defined the shape of the cross as one related to the swastika. ultimately, there is intended to be a portrayal of what cannot typically be portrayed—"the . . . relation between the Divine and the Universe."[60]

there's a lot to be desired in shifting from the patriarchal defini-tion of *sacrifice* as being an act of giving up a personal state of being or resource in order to facilitate another's, typically a broader, more powerful human-designed system, well-being, or success. there is an implication that the state of consciousness required to perform such a gesture is one of enlightenment if we can step out of or overcome

---

59   Elia Diane Fushi Bekene, *Ancestral Tarot* (Flower Press, 2022).
60   Arthur Edward Waite, *The Pictorial Key to the Tarot* (William Rider & Son, 1911).

our "baser" more defensive animal instincts in order to serve a more detached higher human "good," which reinforces the hierarchical structure explored earlier.

Rachel Pollack explored the capacity of the Hanged Man to tap into Jung's collective unconscious, as referenced earlier, and described this image of a male figure hanging from the ankle as "a young initiate in some secret tradition." she went on to describe the tree within the Hanged Man as a representation of the "conscious mind's connection to the wisdom and life energy of the unconscious" and further clarified that the Hanged Man is a powerful representation of the connection between the conscious, the subconscious, and the unconscious[61]—a perfect opportunity, then, to decenter the human form from this image and to allow natural process to embody the journey entailed in this card.

if we instead explore this as an act of *surrender*, we strip this narrative and expose the natural inclinations beneath to give space to the cyclical changes that we as creatures are designed to move through. The chrysalis is similarly anchored to the branch of the tree as an act of stabilizing by rooting through the infinite knowledge of the earth. the journey of the caterpillar through its chrysalis phase is a perfect portrayal of one of nature's most mysterious transformations into the butterfly. a process of nebulization, moving into the chrysalis is an act of surrender to the processes buried within the unconscious that require full stillness to unfold. one piece of Waite's descriptions does resonate and feels appropriate here, which is that the caterpillar, through no instruction outside of itself, is aware at its core that "the story of [its] higher nature is embedded in this symbolism,"[62] and indeed is embedded within its primal blueprints. Pollack described the Hanged Man energy as one of *independence*, in the sense that we must go through our own inner processes of differentiation and divergence—to create a boundary in which

---

61 Rachel Pollack, *Seventy-Eight Degrees of Wisdom: A Book of Tarot* (Weiser Books, 2019), 298.
62 Waite, *The Pictorial Key to the Tarot*.

we are able to safely unravel and transform—in order to return to a state of being "deeply connected to life."[63]

the loss described in *surrender* is not just one of a previous state of being, but also the process that occurs naturally in any transformative process, in which some materials from the original form must be lost in order to take new shape. recentering this process away from one of *human strife*—as though we are the only conscious beings who can *rise above* the state of being human to being god-like—into the natural process of retreating from one's environment in order to catalyze deep growth can draw comparisons to the cycles of hibernation, a process we recognize to be critical to restoring one's resources and energies. as patriarchy and capitalism currently prevent us from accessing this natural cyclical way of being, this card may in fact represent the breakdown we experience when our outer world can't slow down to facilitate what needs to unfold within the inner landscape. CHRYSALIS, we can see, reveals to us one of the most critical layers of *queering*, in which we surrender our current understanding of our universe in exchange for an entirely new perspective.

---

63   Pollack, *Seventy-Eight Degrees of Wisdom*, 100.

And With That...

This book does not conclude or finalize any ideas of queerness, tarot, or spirituality. That was never my goal. My goal with *Tarot in Other Words* was to bring some of my absolute favorite queer tarot voices together to bring you new ideas, techniques, and inspiration for your own journeys. I wanted to see a tarot book in essay form, with a number of different voices, each providing something unique that together would create something beautiful. I wanted to make a harmony of a tarot book.

What my collaborators have brought to this project hit that goal and brought more life, personality, and juiciness to the tarot conversation than anyone could have dreamt of. What together we have provided is one of many resources that you will hopefully return to time and time again, noticing or taking away something different each time. Tarot tells stories, and it is high time we begin using it to tell our own instead of the ones being handed down since the 1400s. Tarot is evergreen—but like an evergreen tree, it is meant to grow. To change. To reach for the sky. To provide beauty for some, practical needs for others, and home for the rest of us.

To do that, we need to keep the tarot conversation going and updating. We need to constantly be questioning what we know, what we think we know, and how it impacts those we are in conversation with. We need to hear new ideas, big ideas, brilliant ideas. We need to know where we come from—a long chosen ancestral lineage of rebels and brick throwers, of lovers and community builders, of artists and philosophers. From there we can decide where we are going. The tarot can help. The tarot will help. What we do with this tool? That is up to us.

APPENDIX

Essayist Bios

Charlie Claire Burgess is a queer and trans-nonbinary writer, illustrator, and witch whose work explores the intersection of spirituality, the occult, and queerness. They are the author of *Radical Tarot* and the author-illustrator of the *Fifth Spirit Tarot* and *Gay Marseille Tarot* decks. Their second book, *Queer Devotion*, an exploration of the queer divine in figures of myth and legend that opens pathways for LGBTQIA+ folks to revere the sacred in themselves, is forthcoming from Hay House in 2025. Charlie's fiction and nonfiction have appeared in *The Lambda Literary Review, F(r)iction, Hunger Mountain,* and elsewhere, and have received a Pushcart Prize Special Mention and notable mentions in two *Best American* anthologies. They have an MFA in creative writing from Vanderbilt University. Born and raised in Alabama, Charlie has made their home in Oregon with their spouse and their one-eyed pug, Apollo. Find them online at *thewordwitchtarot.com* and on Instagram @the.word.witch.

Asali Earthwork is a Black queer femme living on land historically stewarded by the Akokisa, Karankawa, Esto'k Gna, Atakapa-Ishak, Coahuiltecan, and Mascogo peoples. She is the author of the *Asali Earthwork* blog, a resource and reflection space dedicated to the practice of radical co-healing as an act of resistance. She is also the creator of the #TarotoftheQTPOC project, which centers and highlights *QTBIPOC Tarot* and *Lenormand* deck creators and their work.

Maria the Arcane, a practicing witch of twenty-three years, discovered her craft in the magickal forests of Germany at the age of thirteen. Now, living in South Carolina with her wife and witchling, she is an avid tarot deck collector and reader, a photographer, and a cohost on the podcast *Coffee & Cauldrons.*

Maria Minnis is an unapologetically Black, Jewish, and queer tarot reader of twenty-plus years who teaches people about blending their spirituality with magic, liberation work, and eroticism in their everyday lives. She believes that the end result of all magic should be to cultivate a more equitable and empathetic planet. Her highly acclaimed antiracism tarot workbook *Tarot for the Hard Work* is available online and in stores. Follow her work on Instagram *@feminnis* and at *mariaminnis.com.*

Junada Petrus's first book, *The Stars and the Blackness Between Them,* received the Coretta Scott King Honor Book Award. She has recently released her first children's book, *Can We Please Give the Police Department to the Grandmothers?* based on her abolitionist love poem. In her performance work as an aerialist, she intertwined her background in Black diaspora dance and explored themes of Blackness reclaimed and reimagined in the vertical space. Her work seeks to heal the legacy of violence and lynching that we associate with "Black bodies swinging." From this, she wrote and directed *There Are Other Worlds,* an ancestral-aerial-circus-poem-play. She has created and performed in her own experimental short film work, including *Love Tones, Out My Mind* and most recently *Erotics of Abolition.* In all her artistic forms, she explores diaspora, the erotic, the speculative, ancestral magic, stories of queerness and femmehood, wildness, laughter, sweetness, spectacle, and shimmer.

Siri Vincent Plouff (*they/them*) is a Nordic witch, rune reader, and tarot reader based on Anishinaabe and Dakota land, aka Minneapolis, Minnesota. As an unabashedly queer person, they are constantly interrogating runes and Nordic practices through a unique lens of gender identity. You can find Siri online at their website, *sirivincentplouff.com*. They share their knowledge of all things heathenry on their podcast, *The Heathen's Journey*. They are in training with Kari Tauring, a modern-day völva. Siri teaches about the runes, tarot, and witchcraft. Their signature course is the Radical Runes Course. Their debut solo book, *Queering the Runes*, published by Weiser Books, is out now. They are also the coauthor of *Lessons from the Empress: A Tarot Workbook for Self-Care and Creative Growth*.

Rebecca (Bee) Scolnick is a writer, witch, weirdo, and queer human lady (*she/her*), who uses magic and storytelling to support the work of unlearning that which you *think* you know, and to inspire new meaning making. Her first book, *The Witch's Book of Numbers: Enhance Your Magic with Numerology*, was released in 2022. She currently lives in Los Angeles with her wife and pup, both of whom she's deeply obsessed with. In addition to her numerology and magical works, she's also a writer of queer romantic comedies. You can connect with her further at *rebeccascolnick.com*, or on social media @beescolnick.

Cassandra Snow (*they/them*) is a writer, tarot professional, and theatre and performance artist. They are the author of *Queering the Tarot*, *Queering Your Craft: Witchcraft from the Margins*, and coauthor of *Lessons from the Empress: A Tarot Workbook for Self-Care and Creative Growth*. In their other life, they are one of the voices on *Lesser Evil: A DnDish Podcast*, and sit on the advisory council for the Flip the Script Film Festival. Learn more about Cassandra, including where to buy their books, at *cassandra-snow.com* or on social media where their handle is usually *mx.cassandra.snow*.

Taylor Ursula weaves together astrology, tarot, and hypnosis to create unique experiences of depth and self-awareness in her one-on-one and group work. her ability to hold divine space is grounded by her practice as a therapist, and she holds a deep curiosity for the human experience. she is the creator of PORTALS, a transcendental and disembodied tarot experience, and creates magical ephemera and tools for naming and marking the path of our journeys. Taylor recently completed her master's degree in clinical psychology at Pepperdine University and is working toward licensure as an LMFT/LPCC.

Meg Jones Wall (*she/they*) is a queer, chronically ill tarot reader and teacher, who creates tarot resources and courses for spiritual misfits through her business, *3am.tarot*. Meg is the author of *Finding the Fool: A Tarot Journey to Radical Transformation,* with two more tarot books forthcoming. They are based in NYC.

Cassandra's Acknowledgments

First and foremost, I want to thank the absolute rock star essayists who contributed to this collection. I am so moved by your work. I learn so much from you all all the time—about tarot, about magic, about queerness and friendship and praxis and and and. I am so unbelievably humbled to have done this project for and with you all. Thank you for saying yes and coming through, and for going so far above and beyond the call of duty within that.

I want to thank my wonderful agent, Kelly Van Sant, as well as the whole team at K.T. Literary. This project is what it is because of you all, and I'm so excited to see where this relationship takes us in the future. I want to thank Kathryn Sky-Peck for her continued impeccable work on editing and design. You are one of my favorite working relationships, and I'm delighted that this one ended up in your hands after all. The whole team at Weiser as it stands now is a delight—thank you to everyone in marketing, sales, editing, and proofreading. Our books would (sometimes literally) fall apart without each and every one of you. I also want to thank Peter Turner for taking a chance on this collection in the first place.

My family, my friends, the many people who fall into both categories. I love you so very much. You all really took the brunt of my fretting, anxiety, and general emotional health on this one, and I know I would have finished this project regardless, but I'm so glad I had you to bounce ideas off of, whine to, and occasionally cry on your shoulder. Thank you. I especially want to thank Manny, Bridget, and the Stolps.

And, of course, none of this would be possible without those who buy, read, and spread the word about my books. Without those who interview me, who review my books, who engage with the work and cite it. Who hire me for tarot readings, classes, and lessons. Who believe in all the weird, kooky things I do and want to see me succeed. Thank you. Thank you. Thank you. Words are not enough, but they're all I've got. (Luckily, I have quite a few of them.)

To Our Readers

Weiser Books, an imprint of Red Wheel/Weiser, publishes books across the entire spectrum of occult, esoteric, speculative, and New Age subjects. Our mission is to publish quality books that will make a difference in people's lives without advocating any one particular path or field of study. We value the integrity, originality, and depth of knowledge of our authors.

Our readers are our most important resource, and we appreciate your input, suggestions, and ideas about what you would like to see published.

Visit our website at *www.redwheelweiser.com*, where you can learn about our upcoming books and free downloads, and also find links to sign up for our newsletter and exclusive offers.

You can also contact us at *info@rwwbooks.com* or at

Red Wheel/Weiser, LLC

65 Parker Street, Suite 7

Newburyport, MA 01950